Addiction in America
Society, Psychology, and Heredity

ILLICIT AND MISUSED DRUGS

ILLICIT AND MISUSED DRUGS

Addiction in America
Society, Psychology, and Heredity

by Ida Walker

Mason Crest

Mason Crest
370 Reed Road
Broomall, Pennsylvania 19008
www.masoncrest.com

Printed in the Hashemite Kingdom of Jordan.

First printing
9 8 7 6 5 4 3 2 1

Library of Congress Cataloging-in-Publication Data

Walker, Ida.
  Addiction in America : society, psychology and heredity / Ida Walker.
     p. cm. — (Illicit and misused drugs)
Includes bibliographical references and index.
ISBN 978-1-4222-2426-7 (hardcover)
ISBN 978-1-4222-2424-3 (series hardcover)
ISBN 978-1-4222-9290-7 (ebook)
1. Substance abuse—United States. 2. Teenagers—Substance use—
United States. 3. Teenagers—Drug use—United States. 4. Teen-
agers—Alcohol use—United States. 5. Addicts—United States.
I. Title.
  HV4999.Y68W355 2012
  362.290973—dc23
                                        2011032550

Interior design by Benjamin Stewart.
Cover design by Torque Advertising + Design.
Produced by Harding House Publishing Services, Inc.
  www.hardinghousepages.com

This book is meant to educate and should not be used as an alternative to ap-
propriate medical care. Its creators have made every effort to ensure that the
information presented is accurate—but it is not intended to substitute for the
help and services of trained professionals.

 **CONTENTS**

INTRODUCTION

Addicting drugs are among the greatest challenges to health, well-being, and the sense of independence and freedom for which we all strive—and yet these drugs are present in the everyday lives of most people. Almost every home has alcohol or tobacco waiting to be used, and has medicine cabinets stocked with possibly outdated but still potentially deadly drugs. Almost everyone has a friend or loved one with an addiction-related problem. Almost everyone seems to have a solution neatly summarized by word or phrase: medicalization, legalization, criminalization, war-on-drugs.

For better and for worse, drug information seems to be everywhere, but what information sources can you trust? How do you separate misinformation (whether deliberate or born of ignorance and prejudice) from the facts? Are prescription drugs safer than "street" drugs? Is occasional drug use really harmful? Is cigarette smoking more addictive than heroin? Is marijuana safer than alcohol? Are the harms caused by drug use limited to the users? Can some people become addicted following just a few exposures? Is treatment or counseling just for those with serious addiction problems?

These are just a few of the many questions addressed in this series. It is an empowering series because it provides the information and perspectives that can help people come to their own opinions and find answers to the challenges posed by drugs in their own lives. The series also provides further resources for information and assistance, recognizing that no single source has all the answers. It should be of interest and relevance to areas of study spanning biology, chemistry, history, health, social studies and more. Its efforts to provide a real-world context for the information that is clearly presented but not overly simplified should be appreciated by students, teachers, and parents.

The series is especially commendable in that it does not pretend to pose easy answers or imply that all decisions can be made on the basis of simple facts: some challenges have no immediate or simple solutions, and some solutions will need to rely as much upon basic values as basic facts. Despite this, the series should help to at least provide a foundation of knowledge. In the end, it may help as much by pointing out where the solutions are not simple, obvious, or known to work. In fact, at many points, the reader is challenged to think for him- or herself by being asked what his or her opinion is.

A core concept of the series is to recognize that we will never have all the facts, and many of the decisions will never be easy. Hopefully, however, armed with information, perspective, and resources, readers will be better prepared for taking on the challenges posed by addictive drugs in everyday life.

— *Jack E. Henningfield, Ph.D.*

7 What Is Addiction?

According to the University of Pennsylvania Health System (www.uphs.upenn.edu), approximately 15 percent of the U.S. population is addicted to alcohol, drugs, or a combination of the two. Another 25 percent are addicted to some form of tobacco. Although that might seem like a small number (after all, that means about 85 percent of people in the United States do *not* have a problem with drugs or alcohol), the costs of addiction are not a small number. These costs show up in substance-related medical conditions (such as hepatitis among those who abuse alcohol, or HIV/AIDS in those who share needles), crime, lost job **productivity**, and treatment. Research estimates that addiction costs the United States almost $600 *billion* each year.

Many of us know someone—often in our own families—who has a problem with drugs, alcohol, or other substances. Often what we don't know, however, is what addiction really is.

Addiction: A Definition

When a drug or other substance is taken into the body, it creates a reaction. When a prescription or over-the-counter drug is taken as instructed by a health-care professional or according to the product label, the effects can be anticipated and are usually desired. These medications are taken to treat a medical condition, and a reaction is what is sought. However, when someone takes them in ways or amounts contrary to their intended use, **adverse** effects—including dependence and addiction—can occur.

The definition of addiction has changed over the years. It was originally used in **pharmacology** to refer to the tolerance-inducing qualities of some drugs and substances. If something has tolerance-inducing qualities, the body gets used to having the substance in its system. When this occurs, the individual must take increasingly larger amounts of the drug to achieve the original effect.

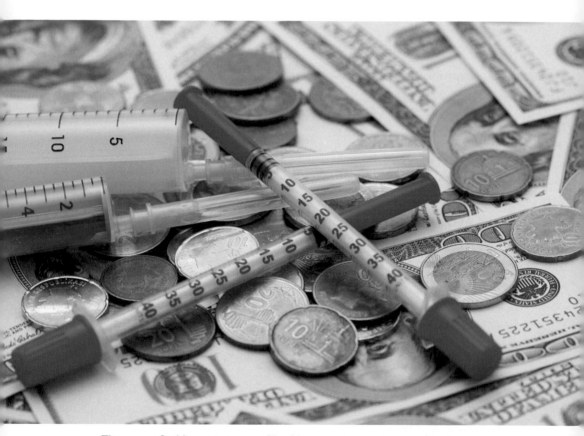

The costs of addiction in terms of health care, crime, and lost productivity are enormous.

Abuse—or Misuse?

Addiction is not the only problem that can arise from substance use. Individuals can abuse and misuse substances as well. Though they are two different things, both can lead to addiction.

Misuse:

Patients may forget or not understand their prescription's directions. They may start making their own decisions, perhaps upping the dose in hopes of getting better faster.

Abuse:

People may use prescription drugs for nonmedical reasons. Prescription drug abusers may obtain such drugs illegally and use them to get high, fight stress, or boost energy.

This definition emphasizes the physiological aspects of taking drugs.

While the pharmacologists had their definition of addiction, the general public was coming up with its own. They took a broader approach to defining addiction. To the general public, addiction referred to someone's *propensity* to keep abusing a substance even though it was clear that it was not good for him; none of the negatives associated with the practice could outweigh the perceived pros of using the substance.

The medical and scientific communities had their own thoughts to add to the definition of addiction. Segments of the medical community adopted the general public's definition as well, and addiction was considered to be a disease state. There are, however, some significant differences in the definition as developed by medicine and science.

The medical and scientific communities make distinctions between physical dependence and psychological dependence (or addiction), and their definitions are relatively narrow. Someone who is physically dependent on a substance will suffer a predictable physiological response should she stop taking the drug suddenly—go "cold turkey." These responses—withdrawal symptoms—can include headaches or agitation. Someone who is psychologically dependent—addicted—to a substance has an uncontrolled, compulsive need to use the drug or other chemical substance. Some characteristics of addiction are:

- impaired control over drug use
- compulsive use
- continued use despite harm
- craving

Not all medical professionals agree on a definition of addiction, however. It was once believed that only *psychoactive* drugs that crossed the **blood–brain barrier** could be considered addictive. These drugs would temporarily change the brain chemistry, giving the person a period of *euphoria*—the high or rush sought by individuals abusing drugs. Today, many people want to add nondrugs such as gambling, food, sex, and pornography to the list of addictive substances.

Proponents of this way of thinking claim that people participating in these behaviors experience a high. They cite studies showing that the **hypothalamus** produces *peptides* when people participate in such activities, just as it does when people use an addictive chemical substance. They further argue that **endorphins** released into

Addiction: A Psychiatric Definition

Addiction is a primary, chronic, neurobiological disease, with genetic, psycho-social, and environmental factors influencing its development and manifestations. It is characterized by behaviors that include one or more of the following: impaired control over drug use, compulsive use, continued use despite harm, and craving.

Addiction is the more widely used term for what the American Psychiatric Association and World Health Organization refer to in their technical and diagnostic documents as "*dependence.*"

the brain when people gamble, eat, or view pornography, among other addictive behaviors, positively reinforce the behavior of the individual who has a problem with these activities. Proponents of this definition also claim that when someone addicted to such behaviors suddenly stops, withdrawal symptoms are encountered, just as they are when someone stops abusing an addictive drug.

Not everyone in the medical field believes that activities such as those listed above are truly addictive since they do not involve any substances that cross the blood–brain barrier. Opponents of the idea of activity addiction do agree that people who have problems with those activities face withdrawal-type effects when they are unable to participate in them. Their contention, however, is that these effects are **symptomatic** of a behavior disorder, not a true addiction.

The term "addiction" does not appear in the *Diagnostic and Statistical Manual of Mental Disorders* (DSM-IV TR, the most recent release). Instead, it mentions physical dependence, abuse, and withdrawal symptoms of drugs. However, the American Psychiatric Association, publisher of the DSM, is contemplating changing the word dependence to addiction in the next edition of the manual.

In reality, addiction can have both physiological and psychological aspects.

Physiological Dependence

As mentioned earlier in this chapter, physical dependence means that the body will go through withdrawal symptoms when the substance is removed. Not all drugs and other chemical substances that produce physiological dependency are addictive. For example, *cortisone*, *beta-blockers*, some laxatives, nasal decongestants, and many antidepressants cause a physical dependency but are not addictive. Although not all prescription drugs are addictive, none should be stopped suddenly without the guidance of a health-care professional.

Psychological Addiction

Human nature makes one want to repeat behaviors that bring pleasure and avoid those that do not. The person who abuses a substance does so despite oftentimes knowing that he is doing something harmful, perhaps even life threatening. But the pleasurable feeling waiting on the other side of taking the substance spurs a psychological need to use that substance that outweighs any risk. It can be just as hard—and sometimes harder—to break this psychological bond than the physical dependence on the substance.

Rather than revise the various definitions of addiction into a single *cohesive* one, the growing trend is not to distinguish between addiction and dependence, opting to use the word addiction to represent both conditions.

Addiction Vocabulary

Abuse: The use of a drug in a manner detrimental to the individual or society but not meeting criteria for addiction or dependence.

Note: Abuse is sometimes used as a synonym for drug abuse, substance abuse, drug addiction, chemical dependency, and substance dependency.

Diversion: The removal of legitimately manufactured controlled medications from lawful, legitimate use into illicit drug trafficking.

Note: Diversion cases involve, but are not limited to, physicians who sell prescriptions to drug dealers or abusers; pharmacists who falsify records and subsequently sell the medications; employees who steal from inventory; executives who falsify orders to cover illicit sales; prescription forgers; and individuals who commit armed robbery of pharmacies and drug distributors.

Misuse: 1) The use of a prescription medication in ways other than how it was prescribed, or 2) the use of an over-the-counter medication contrary to approved labeling unless taken as directed by a healthcare provider, and below the threshold of abuse.

Nonmedical use: The use of a prescription medication in a manner inconsistent with accepted medical practice, or the use of an over-the-counter medication contrary to approved labeling.

Physical dependence: Physical dependence is a state of adaptation that is manifested by a drug class specific withdrawal syndrome that can be produced by abrupt cessation, rapid dose reduction, decreasing blood level of drug and/or administration of an antagonist and is relieved by the readministration of the drug or another drug of the same pharmacologic class.

Recovery: A process of overcoming both physical and psychological dependence on a psychoactive substance, with a commitment to a drug free state. This is frequently referred to as a commitment to "sobriety" emphasizing the fact that the terminology has its roots

Continued on following page.

more in alcohol treatment and it emphasizes the life-long nature of the process.

Tolerance: Tolerance is a state of adaptation in which exposure to a drug induces changes that result in a diminution of one or more of the drug's effects over time. A need for markedly increased amounts of the drug to achieve intoxication or desired effects, or markedly diminished effects with continued use of the same amount of the drug.

Withdrawal: A constellation of symptoms that can follow rapid discontinuation of daily use of most addictive drugs with symptoms differing across drugs but frequently including withdrawal or a tendency to resume drug taking.

Withdrawal can occur in people who do not show other signs of addiction, such as pain patients on opioids who stop taking their medicines, or babies borne by addicted mothers.

Signs of Addiction

Some people can use alcohol and other substances without much of a problem. They know how much they can handle and when to stop. When they aren't using the substances, they suffer no withdrawal symptoms.

So how can one tell if an individual has a problem with substance abuse and addiction? In many cases, it depends on the type of drug being used, but according to the website Addictions.org, there are some common signs of substance abuse:

- change in friends; hanging out with a new group
- reclusive behavior—long periods spent in self-imposed isolation
- long, unexplained absences

- lying and stealing
- involvement on the wrong side of the law
- deteriorating family relationships
- obvious intoxication, delirious, incoherent or unconscious
- changes in behavior and attitude
- decrease in school performance

If someone exhibits some of those characteristics, it doesn't always mean that the individual has an addiction or substance abuse problem. However, the possibility should be examined. Should someone have a problem with drugs or alcohol, it is important that he receives help. Choosing the right treatment method often depends on how the individual became addicted.

How People Become Addicted

Someone doesn't just wake up one day and decide he is going to develop an addiction or dependency. Addiction doesn't work that way; it is a process, not a spur-of-the-moment decision. For most people, using drugs—including alcohol, tobacco, and prescription and over-the-counter medications—is not a physical or psychological problem when they are used sparingly. For other people, the drug or other substance becomes the overwhelming force driving all their actions. Life becomes centered on getting and using the substance being abused.

Why one person develops an addiction to a substance while another person using the same substance doesn't, remains pretty much a mystery. *Hypotheses* abound for the causes of addiction, however. The most common theories are based on society, psychology, and heredity.

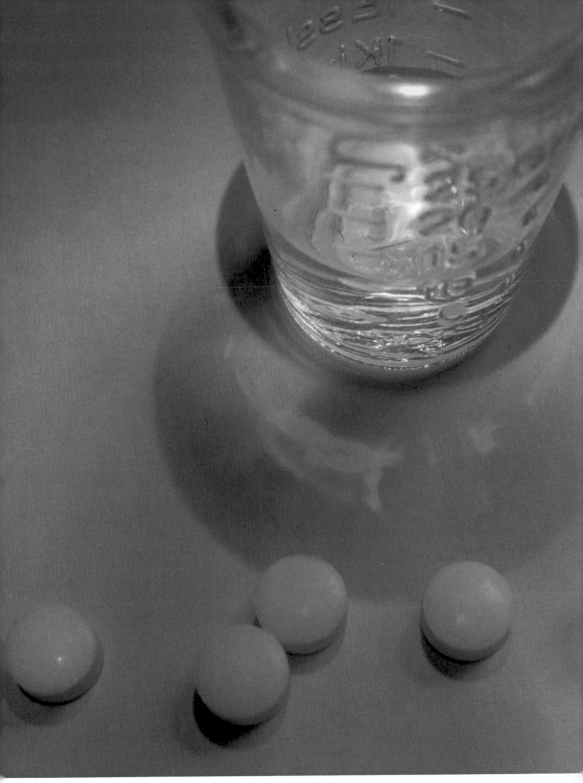

Addiction is a process that takes time; many people do not realize they have a problem until it is already a serious one.

Chapter 1—What Is Addiction?

For some, addiction may arise from society and the social pressures, including peer pressure, common to everyday life. Some researchers believe addiction has a psychological cause. Proponents of this theory believe that there is something in the individual's psychological makeup that can lead to addiction. Other researchers have found that there may be a genetic *predisposition* to developing an addiction, especially to alcohol. This doesn't mean that the child of an alcoholic will definitely become an alcoholic, just that there might be an increased chance that this could happen.

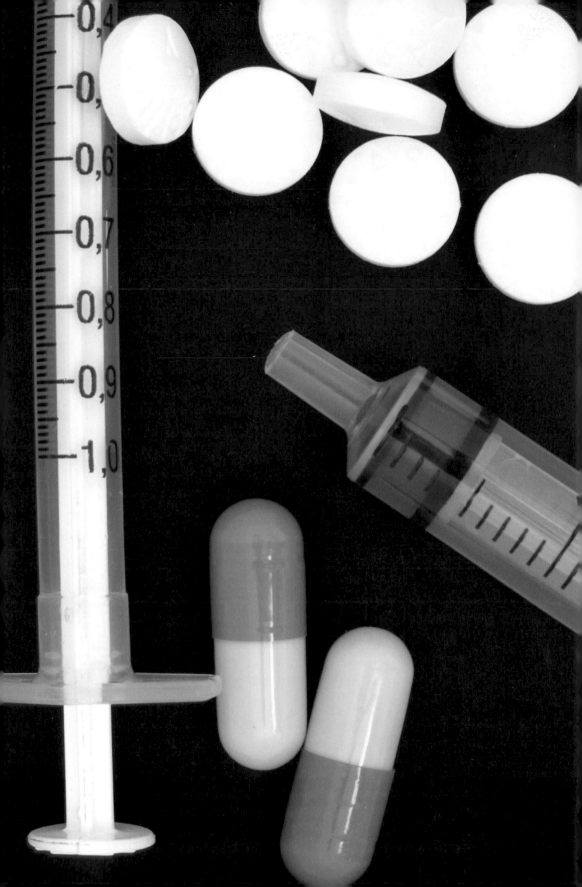

2 Society, Culture, and Addiction

Maggie is seventeen years old. She has two older sisters, both prettier, more intelligent, and more popular than she is. At least that's Maggie's opinion. She doesn't think she can become prettier or smarter, but she thought she could do something about her popularity quotient.

That's why when Maggie started high school, she dropped most the friends she had had since elementary school. She hadn't gotten popular with them as friends, so they must be the reason for her unpopularity, she figured. Maggie started hanging out with some juniors, who seemed to know where all the really fun parties were. She also started drinking—a lot.

One thing all the cool kids had in common was that they drank. So, because she definitely wanted to be a cool kid, Maggie decided she would drink, too. At first it was only on Friday nights when she went out with friends. Then she started going out on Saturday, too, and having a drink—or two, maybe three if it were a special occasion. And Maggie got her wish; she is popular now.

Now, her junior year of high school, it's hard for her to remember when she wasn't drinking. Weekend drinking expanded; she and her friends started on Thursday and sometimes got together on Sunday to knock back a few. Though Maggie enjoyed being with her friends, she now found that they weren't necessary to having a good time. Her parents kept beer in the refrigerator, and Maggie got very clever at drinking it without her parents knowing. She could stay home and not have to share.

Were there any downsides to Maggie's new friends and "hobby"? Well, she noticed that her fingernails broke off a lot, and her hair seemed kind of brittle, almost scraggly. Oh, and sometimes she had a real killer headache and her stomach was upset. But her friends didn't mind, and, after all, she was popular!

Maggie's story is a **composite** one based on conversations that occurred in an Internet chat room. Maggie and others like her become addicted to a substance—in her case, alcohol—because of society and the pressures it puts on individuals. Ours is a fast-paced, highly competitive world, and many people find they cannot cope without a little extra help, a little boost. Others may need help dealing with loss or disappointment, other significant components of today's world. While some people might find help through yoga, meditation and other relaxation techniques, or exercise, others will turn to alcohol, tobacco, and other substances.

Alcohol addiction is very common in our society.

Smoking is one of the most common teen addictions.

24 Chapter 2—Society, Culture, and Addiction

The Influence of Others: Parents and Peers

The teenage years are a time when teenagers often explore themselves and the world around them. Though these years help plant the seeds for future adulthood and its responsibilities, they are meant to be fun. For most teens, it's a period when their parents give them a bit more freedom; they loosen the reins. Teens are allowed (and even encouraged) to make more of their own decisions, especially when it comes to matters that affect them most directly. Teens are also expected to cope with the consequences of those decisions.

For many, the newfound exploration and freedom includes learning to drive, getting a job, and dating. For some, their new freedoms also mean experimenting with drugs and other substances. If the teen's **peer group** includes individuals who abuse drugs or alcohol—like the group Maggie began hanging out with—there is a definite increase in the possibility of substance abuse. For some, experimenting with substances is short lived; for others, it signals the beginning of a pattern of addiction.

How an individual deals with drugs and alcohol is a learned behavior taught by a variety of teachers. Parents are the first, and in many ways the most important, teachers an individual will ever have. If parents abuse alcohol, tobacco, or other drugs, that behavior becomes an acceptable part of their children's environment. These children may come to believe that drugs and alcohol are the only way to deal with unpleasant situations or even to celebrate joyous occasions. Substance use becomes their normal. Substance abuse can become a pattern of everyday life.

Even parents or siblings who take prescription medications according to instructions can facilitate drug abuse

Drug Approval

Before a drug can be marketed in the United States, the Food and Drug Administration (FDA) must officially approve it. Today's FDA is the primary consumer protection agency in the United States. Operating under the authority given it by the government, and guided by laws established throughout the twentieth century, the FDA has established a rigorous drug approval process that verifies the safety, effectiveness, and accuracy of labeling for any drug marketed in the United States.

While the United States has the FDA for the approval and regulation of drugs and medical devices, Canada has a similar organization called the Therapeutic Product Directorate (TPD). The TPD is a division of Health Canada, the Canadian government's department of health. The TPD regulates drugs, medical devices, disinfectants, and sanitizers with disinfectant claims. Some of the things that the TPD monitors are quality, effectiveness, and safety. Just as the FDA must approve new drugs in the United States, the TPD must approve new drugs in Canada before those drugs can enter the market.

in teens. Some of the fastest-growing drugs of choice for young people are prescription drugs. Many homes have at least one type of prescription medication in their medicine cabinets, making it easily available for abuse. Teens and young adults may be under the misconception that because the U.S. Food and Drug Administration (FDA) or the Therapeutic Product Directorate (TPD) in Canada has approved the medication, and a health-care professional prescribes it, then it is safe for everyone to use. That is a potentially fatal misunderstanding.

Next to parents, peers are probably the most important influences on a teen's life. As the child becomes an adolescent and then a young adult, peer group influence becomes increasingly important at each developmental stage. The influence of friends does not begin during the teen years, however. During their middle-school years,

Teens' decisions are often influenced by their peers.

kids begin to expand their lives away from their families, and friends become a bigger influence on their way of thinking and acting. As the child continues to evolve as a young adult, away from the core family, the importance of her peers' opinions increases. She tends to look to her friends for advice on how to dress, what music to listen to, and what films and television shows to watch. Friends also influence how the teen behaves, including whether to abuse substances.

Advertisements in the media have often portrayed smoking as glamorous and relaxing.

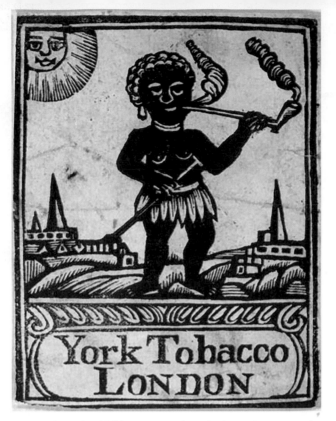

A tobacco label from the 1600s portrays the role that tobacco was beginning to play in English and colonial life.

As mentioned earlier, involvement with a peer group that emphasizes substance abuse can make that behavior seem commonplace and a way to be popular. (Remember Maggie?) Most people want to have friends, and for some teens, being popular and drinking alcohol, smoking, or abusing drugs is their way of finding that popularity.

Not all peer groups have a negative influence on their members. Individuals whose peer groups are made up of academically inclined or sports-minded members, for example, are generally less inclined to abuse substances.

The Influence of the Media

How many homes in the United States and Canada do not have a television or computer, or get a newspaper or magazine at least occasionally? That number has to be miniscule. The media is everywhere, and it is a major influence on behavior, especially that of children and adolescents. Between television, films, computers, music, and video, images of substance abuse abound. Young people spend hours in front of computers and television sets, so it is understandable if some begin to believe that abusing substances is an acceptable (in some cases, perhaps preferable) way to have fun or to deal with stress and other life conditions. Films, song lyrics, and music videos can reinforce that idea in a young person's mind.

Media's influence isn't limited to television programs and magazine articles, however. Advertising has a phenomenal influence on behavior, including that of teens. Businesses know the power they have over the buying patterns of teens and adults, and they take full advantage of every opportunity they have—or can create. One of the most effective uses of advertising and the media to influence behavior is in the marketing of tobacco and the smoking lifestyle.

The Case of Tobacco

Tobacco use predates European settlement in either the United States or Canada. The popularity of cigarettes really didn't come into its own, however, until World War I. Soldiers were encouraged to smoke cigarettes as an antidote for the stresses encountered in battle. On the homefront, the number of women who smoked cigarettes increased. Before the war, women were not inclined to look upon individuals who smoked with much more than disgust. Tobacco products were considered vulgar, and smoking was a dirty habit "proper" individuals—

That's the merriest Christmas any smoker can have—
Chesterfield mildness plus no unpleasant after-taste

Ronald Reagan

CHESTERFIELD *Buy the beautiful Christmas-card carton*

Advertisers used celebrities to endorse the use of tobacco.

Even in the early years of television and movies, teens made up a large percentage of viewers. When Laurel and Hardy were shown smoking, teenagers were influenced to do likewise.

especially women—would have no part of. As women fought for and eventually won the right to vote, however, many began looking at the cigarette differently. Instead of being an object met with disdain, cigarettes and smoking became a symbol of equality and freedom; men smoked, and so women had that right as well—anything men could do, so could they. Once a few women began smoking, more and more women took up the habit as a result of what can be called World War I–era peer pressure.

With many women now believing that smoking was a symbol of equality, the tobacco industry looked to the world of fashion to increase their consumer base. Thin was "in" during the Roaring Twenties, and then (as now), women often used smoking as an appetite suppressant. Now, women had two reasons to smoke—to symbolize their equality with men and to stay thin. And tobacco companies were very happy to help these women fill their cigarette "needs." One of the most popular cigarettes of the time was Lucky Strike. Magazine ads for those cigarettes urged women to "Reach for a Lucky Instead of a Sweet."

In the 1930s, famous people were shown smoking tobacco products. President Franklin D. Roosevelt, Babe Ruth, Clark Gable, Humphrey Bogart, and Bette Davis were often shown smoking. Then, as now, celebrity endorsements could bring in big bucks to a company, and tobacco companies rushed to get celebrities to associate their names and faces with a particular product. Rita Hayworth, Rosalind Russell, and Betty Grable were the Lindsay Lohan, Jennifer Lopez, and Mandy Moore of the 1930s (at least in popularity), and cigarette ads featured Hayworth, Russell, and Grable—examples of the era's

Lucky Strike cigarettes encouraged women to consider cigarettes as a healthy alternative to sweets.

ideal of the perfect female shape—smoking slender cigarettes that echoed their thin figures.

All right, the tobacco industry had gone after the male and female adult markets. What was left? Ah yes, that would be the adolescent and young adult consumer. Tobacco companies were determined to market their products to be attractive and "cool" to younger people. And how would they reach that target market? They would go where the adolescents and young adults were—or rather, to what they watch: television and film.

I'm your best friend—
I am your Lucky Strike

am a better friend than hers, for I am made only of ld, fragrant, expensive cen-leaves. Not a single sharp leaf nor a single coarse

bottom leaf mars my good taste or my uniform mildness. I do not irritate your throat. I am, indeed, a soothing companion, the best of friends.

LUCKIES USE ONLY CENTER LEAVES . . . CENTER LEAVES GIVE YOU THE MILDEST SMOKE

They Taste Better

Another early ad for Lucky Strikes also appealed to women smokers.

A 1950 cigarette ad used actor Bing Crosby to encourage smoking.

If you watch reruns of television programs from the 1950s and 1960s, you'll notice that many of the characters are shown smoking. Even some newscasters smoked on air. In an interview shortly before his death from lung cancer in 2005, *ABC News* anchor Peter Jennings expressed his shock at seeing himself smoking on camera during field reports. The 2005 film *Good Night and Good Luck* told the story of one of the most important newscasters in history—Edward R. Morrow—and in true-to-life scenes, Morrow is shown as the ***consummate*** chain smoker.

Smoking also figured prominently in film. Hardly a film was made in which the actors and actresses didn't smoke. Smoking had quickly become part of the entertainment culture, and through culture, society. For a few years, it seemed as though the tide had turned when it came to smoking in movies. However, more recently, alarms have been raised that the incidents of smoking shown on film have increased, thereby influencing more children and teens to smoke. In November 2006, the tobacco giant Philip Morris issued a statement that seemed to agree. Citing studies that show children are influenced to smoke by showing it in films, Philip Morris asked that their tobacco products no longer be featured in movies.

Until 1971, tobacco companies were allowed to pitch their products on television and radio in the United States. It didn't matter what time a program was on, tobacco advertisers saw it as an opportunity to market their products. When the Federal Trade Commission (FTC) ruled that tobacco products could no longer be advertised on television, manufacturers turned to other ways to get their product before the purchasing public. Magazine ads got bigger and more colorful. Billboards ***touting*** one tobacco brand over another punctuated the scenery along U.S. roadways.

In 1998, tobacco advertisements were banned from billboards also, so magazine ads became more important to tobacco companies. And it wasn't just adults who paid attention to these ads. Children had access to the magazines and to the cartoon-like images such as Joe Camel used to sell tobacco products. In many cases, magazines printed tobacco ads beside articles warning readers about harmful chemicals in foods and medicines, endorsing one deadly product while condemning another.

Tobacco companies also turned to sports as an effective marketing tool. Sports are big business, and entire television networks are devoted to it. Star athletes become role models for many young people, who sometimes go to extremes to *emulate* the most successful ones. For a long time, the tobacco industry had its finger in the sports entertainment pie and through celebrity endorsements was able to get its products in front of children and adolescents. And it wasn't just cigarettes that the tobacco industry was using athletes to advertise. Before such ads were prohibited on television, popular commercials included ones in which star baseball players talked about putting "just a pinch between my cheek and gum." That pinch was chewing tobacco, and the use of that product skyrocketed among young amateur baseball players, though the commercials deserve only part of the "credit." These revered athletes were often shown chewing and spitting during nationally televised games.

Another way the tobacco industry worked itself into sports was through sponsorships, both of sporting events and of individual athletes. Putting on a sporting event takes lots of money. Of course, it can also bring an enormous return on the company's investment. During the

Winfield tobacco recommends loudly and clearly that sports spectators use its products!

early days of women's professional tennis, it was difficult for the tour to find a sponsor. Companies knew that increasing numbers of girls and women were playing tennis, and athletes with names like Billie Jean King, Chris Evert, Virginia Wade, Evonne Goolagong, and Rosie Casals were gaining fans. But the great unknown was whether large numbers of people would pay to watch a professional tennis tournament. Enter Philip Morris and their thin cigarette marketed to women. Emblazoned prominently on promotional ads and during matches was the name Virginia Slims. As the popularity of women's tennis grew, so did the number of women exposed to Virginia Slims cigarettes.

Meanwhile, auto racing has been one of the fastest-growing sports in the United States. And among the forms of auto racing, stock-car racing—NASCAR—has grown the fastest and the most. Not only did the numbers

Stock car drivers became moving advertisements for tobacco companies.

"...not a creature was stirring..."

(None, save the doctor going out on a call.)

You remember how it starts—that beloved old Christmas poem:

'Twas the night before Christmas, when all through the house Not a creature was stirring,—not even a mouse.

Well, that isn't always true for the doctor. Sometimes there's just no rest at all for him—even on Christmas Eve. Blizzard or heat wave... December or July... night or day... near or far... no matter when you call, he comes!

According to a recent nationwide survey:

MORE DOCTORS SMOKE CAMELS THAN ANY OTHER CIGARETTE

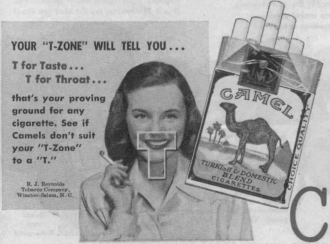

YOUR "T-ZONE" WILL TELL YOU...

T for Taste...
T for Throat...

that's your proving ground for any cigarette. See if Camels don't suit your "T-Zone" to a "T."

R. J. Reynolds
Tobacco Company,
Winston-Salem, N. C.

● Not a single branch of medicine was overlooked in this nationwide survey made by three leading independent research organizations. To 113,597 doctors from Canada to Mexico, from the Atlantic to the Pacific went the query — *What cigarette do you smoke, Doctor?*
The brand named most was Camel.

Like anyone else, a doctor smokes for pleasure. He appreciates rich, full flavor and cool mildness just as any other smoker. If you don't happen to be a Camel smoker now, try Camels. Let your "T-Zone" give you the answer.

Camels *Costlier Tobaccos*

In the 1940s, cigarette companies even used doctors to endorse their products as healthful!

Tobacco has traveled a long road in North America—from a Native American sacred plant to one of the United States' biggest industries, from being used with reverence and prayer to becoming a source of addiction and disease.

of people who went to the races increase, but so did the number of people who watched the races on television and followed the sport's exploits in magazines. During most of stock-car racing's formative years, R. J. Reynolds was the sponsor of NASCAR races—the big leagues. Racing fans throughout the country watched and waited to see who would win the coveted Winston Cup, signifying the racing league's championship. But that wasn't the only way tobacco companies got their product before racing fans. During interviews, people at home had a front-row seat to the phenomenon known as, "driver as walking and talking billboard." Uniforms were often covered with logos from tobacco companies, and it sometimes seemed to be a contest to see which driver could mention his sponsors the most. These sponsors included tobacco companies.

Eventually, faced with public pressure, the federal government stepped in. Research studies indicated that such high-profile sponsorships influenced tobacco use in children and adolescents. In its continuing attempt to limit tobacco's influence on this audience through media, the federal government ruled that tobacco companies could no longer sponsor major, high-profile sporting events. This meant that the women's professional tennis tour and NASCAR, among others, had to seek financing alternatives.

Has the ban been effective on curtailing tobacco use? Many researchers claim it is too early to tell.

Without a doubt, social factors influence the use, abuse, and misuse of illicit substances. Not everyone, however, agrees to what extent society plays a role. Others believe that psychology plays a major role in addiction.

3 Psychology and Addiction

Sam had looked forward to starting high school. His parents had extended his curfew, so that he could go to parties and participate in other activities that come with being a high school student. He had always stuck to his earlier curfew, got good grades, and had friends his parents liked; neither his parents nor Sam saw any reason to think that things would change just because he was going to high school.

Things started out fine for Sam. He liked his classes and even made a few new friends. But after the first few days, once his classes *really* started, Sam found that he had a difficult time keeping up. Subjects that had been easy for him in junior high were now hard. And the teachers seemed to go over things so quickly. There were so many kids in his classes that there wasn't much of a chance to get individual help.

It didn't take long before Sam was lost. He had no idea how this happened. *How can things change so much? Did I get stupid over the summer? All I did was start high school.* As questions like these consumed his thoughts, he began avoiding his friends. His new curfew, the one he had looked forward to for so long, didn't matter, because he came home and went straight to his room every day after school.

Before long, Sam's appetite went away, and sometimes he didn't even want to get out of bed. A few times he even faked being sick so he could stay home. It was during one of those times that Sam found what he thought was a solution to his problem—his parents' liquor cabinet.

It first happened on one of Sam's "fake sick" days home from school. *What am I going to do? I keep getting more and more behind. My parents are going to kill me.*

Sam had been feeling more depressed with each passing day. On this particular day, while his parents were still at work, he wandered over to the liquor cabinet. *Hey, everyone seems to feel so much better after having a drink. Why not?* So Sam took a drink, then another. *Wow! I can't believe how much better I feel.* He started giggling; everything was funny. *Well, now I know how to beat this depression—a good stiff drink!*

Did those drinks cure Sam's depression? No, of course not, but they did make him feel better—for now. Sam, who told his story in an Internet chat room, is like many individuals who become addicted to substances. He has a psychological condition that led to his involvement with alcohol. Though most experts in the addiction field acknowledge that psychology has a role in developing an addiction, there is disagreement about what exactly that role is.

Dual Diagnosis and Self-Medication

One of the most commonly accepted hypotheses about addiction and psychology is the dual diagnosis theory. Proponents of the dual diagnosis hypothesis believe that addiction behavior is a sign of an underlying psychological disorder. Individuals use substances as a self-medication

Individuals often self-medicate: they drink or use drugs to "treat" their depression.

Our culture has come to associate alcohol and good times.

technique. When you do something that makes you feel good, you want to do it again, right? That is the *rationale* behind the theory that self-medication plays a role in addiction. The more pleasurable that experience or feeling is, the more intense is the desire to use the substance again. Sam was depressed, so he drank alcohol. The emotional pain left him. So he is perhaps more inclined to drink alcohol again. In a sense, he "prescribed" alcohol to treat his depression. The problem with that? Well, first, he's not a doctor; second, the alcohol won't make his problems at school go away; and perhaps most important, the pleasurable effects of alcohol come with a price—alcoholism, health issues, and social and legal problems.

Alcohol isn't the only substance that is abused through the practice of self-medication. Some may find marijuana relieves anxiety and makes them feel more sociable. Anxiety, stress, depression, or trauma may cause individuals to develop sleep disturbances; doctors often prescribe sedatives and other medications to treat these disorders. If an individual finds that these medications are effective, but the health-care professional decides they are no longer indicated, the person may find alternative methods of obtaining the drugs, or turn to other substances for the same effect, long past the medical need for the drug.

Like many other drugs, the body may develop a tolerance to alcohol, requiring that the individual consume increasing amounts of the substance to achieve the same effect. For Sam, this means that he'll probably have to

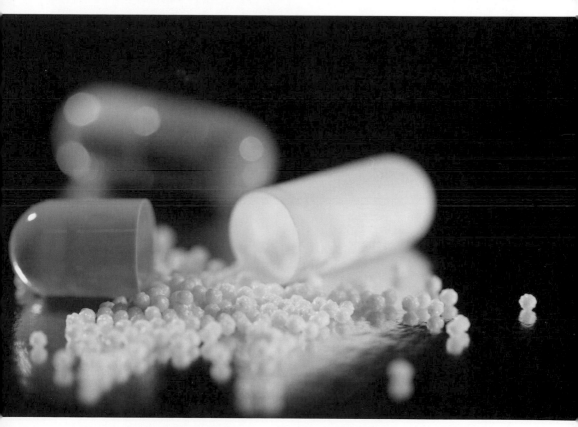

Some addictions begin as legitimate medicinal use—and then, once the medical condition is over, cross the line into dependence.

Some people turn to marijuana to relieve anxiety and stress.

drink more and more often to feel the same relief that his first drinks brought to him.

The dual diagnosis hypothesis is not universally accepted. Those who do not agree completely with this addiction theory cite the fact that many who develop abuse and addiction problems do not have psychological disorders. Others argue that psychological disorders, such as *paranoia*, develop *after* the individual becomes addicted to a substance, especially if the addiction has gone on for a long time. It's the chicken-and-egg argument of addiction research.

The Addictive Personality

Studies have shown that individuals who grow up with alcoholic parents may be more inclined to develop a problem with alcohol or other substances. The question is why? Do these individuals develop addictions because of a genetic quality, because they were exposed to it and perhaps find it socially acceptable, or do they have an addictive personality? In truth, it could be a matter of all three, though the addictive personality concept is more *controversial*.

Many researchers who support the idea of a psychological cause of addiction believe there is an addictive personality. Proponents believe that if the addictive personality could be defined and identified, addictions could be avoided and more effective treatment methods used. They also believe that it is the addictive personality that causes many individuals with addictions to drugs to turn to other forms of addiction after what was considered to be a successful recovery from the drug addiction. Some of the more common post-recovery addictions include gambling, sex, food, and even work.

Most of the research on addictive personality has involved individuals with alcohol addiction. Studies have not proven the existence of such a predisposed personality. Instead, the research supported the fact that many individuals with addictions have no apparent psychological disorders, and those with alcohol addiction do not psychologically differ in any appreciable manner from those who do not.

Other Psychological Causes

Sam knew something was wrong, that he was depressed. Not everyone with a psychological disorder, however, realizes there is something wrong. In that case, they may need help understanding what is going on in their own minds.

Some researchers who favor a psychological cause of addiction believe that addictive behavior is caused by conflicts occurring within the individual on the unconscious level. For example, an individual may exhibit addictive behavior as a defense mechanism against aggression of which the individual is not aware. Others believe that *repressed memories* can also be the cause of addictive behaviors. In either case, addiction is *hypothesized* to be a psychological coping mechanism, although obviously not a favorable one. Unlike other areas of research, little evidence supports that these are actual causes of addiction.

In the ever-growing body of research about addiction, psychological causes are but one area currently being investigated. Alongside psychological causes, heredity is also being closely examined for its role in addiction.

Repressed Memories

Sometimes things happen that are just too painful to remember. When that happens, the mind may repress the memory, push it so far into the subconscious that the individual has no recollection of the event.

Though most psychologists and psychiatrists agree that this might occur, several question that it does as often as one may be led to believe through news accounts and made-for-TV movies. But the severest criticism surrounds how these memories are recalled. In most cases, repressed memories have come to the surface during psychological therapy for some disorder, sometimes addiction. Sometimes the memories surface as a natural part of delving into the individual's subconscious. Other times, they surface through the use of hypnosis; in the hands of ethical psychologists and psychiatrists, this can be a useful treatment tool. However, in the hands of those with an agenda of their own that goes beyond helping the patient, repressed memories—however they are evoked—can bring even more pain to the patient and his or her family.

Most media coverage of repressed memories centers around the results of those recovered memories. In some cases, children have recalled incidents of abuse. In states with liberal statutes of limitations for such crimes, the perpetrator can then be prosecuted. Where it is too late for prosecution, the individual who lived the abuse may be able to reach some resolution by confronting the abuser.

Not all cases have positive outcomes, and those stories also get media attention. In one case, a woman "recalled" seeing her father kill one of her playmates when she was a child. Her father was put on trial and found guilty of the decades-old murder, despite only circumstantial evidence other than his daughter's story. Later, however, as the result of more therapy, this time with a different therapist, it was discovered that the recovered memory was false, an idea planted into her mind by her therapist. Her father was freed, but his reputation had been irreparably damaged.

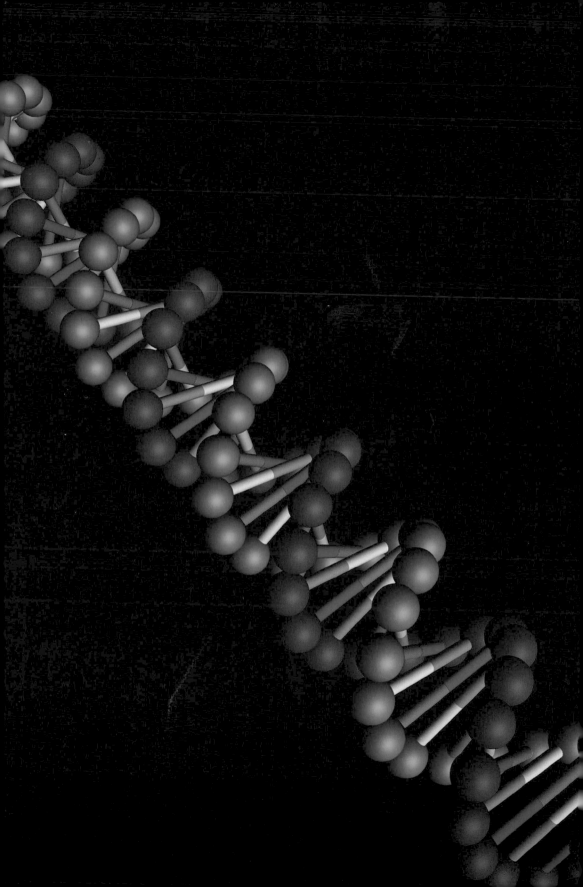

4 Heredity and Addiction

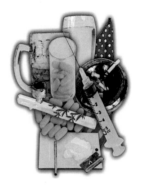

"My mom used to get drunk every weekend. I don't know why she was surprised when I started drinking." (Emma, age fifteen)

"I'm scared to smoke, and it's not because of those anti-tobacco ads they're always showing on TV. I'm afraid that if I try just one, I'll get hooked. My mom and dad both smoke like chimneys, and now my dad will probably die of lung cancer." (Nick, age twelve)

"Well, I don't know why everyone was so shocked when I started using crack. Cripes, my parents, my uncles, and my cousins all get high. Wasn't I doomed from the beginning?" (Antoine, age seventeen)

These are the voices heard in an Internet chat room during a discussion on addiction. Despite differences in gender, age, and drug of choice, they all shared something in common—at least one blood relative who was also addicted to substances.

So if a relative is addicted to a substance, does that mean Antoine is right to think he might have been destined to an addiction to drugs? Is it all a matter of our genes?

What Are Genes?

Most of us share at least a few characteristics with other members of our family. Perhaps it's eye color or the color and texture of our hair. Or maybe it's our ear for music or talent for sports. Whatever it is, genes are the source of those similarities. Simply put, genes transmit the characteristics that all living things—plants and animals—pass from one generation to another. They are the *purveyors* of heredity.

As recently as the 1990s, it was believed that each human had approximately 100,000 genes. That number was slashed to 35,000 as results began to come in from the Human Genome Project. When the project's results were announced in 2004, the number of genes in the human body was further reduced to between 20,000 and 25,000, just over twice the number of genes of the much smaller fruit fly.

Genes are contained in the body's cells, lined up along chromosomes. Chromosomes are threadlike in appearance, and each chromosome is made up of hundreds or thousands of genes. Chromosomes come in pairs, half from the mother and half from the father. Genes and chromosomes are made up of deoxyribonucleic acid, better known as DNA. Everyone's DNA is unique, except for that of identical twins.

The Human Genome Project

In 1990, the U.S. Department of Energy and the National Institutes of Health joined forces to:

- identify the genes in human DNA
- determine the sequence of the 3 billion chemical base pairs that make up human DNA
- store the information in databases
- improve tools for analysis
- transfer related technologies to the private sector
- address the ethical, legal, and social issues that arose from the project.

In 2003, it completed its task. Throughout its thirteen-year history, the United Kingdom, Japan, France, Germany, and China were among the countries that provided support for the study, making it a truly international effort.

The ambitious program helped identify genes responsible for some health issues. For example, the gene believed to be responsible for breast cancer was one of those pinpointed by the study's research.

Despite the health benefits that could arise from such a study, the Human Genome Project was not without controversy. Concerns were raised that the information learned from the research could be used to facilitate such practices as cloning and genetic engineering.

Although human genes have now been mapped and the project completed, work has not ended. It is expected that it will take many years to analyze all of the data obtained through the Human Genome Project.

The Job of the Genes

Everything in our body has a role, a purpose, a job to do. The job of the genes is to carry instructions on chemically making proteins in the cell. Scientists believe that each gene may be responsible for creating up to ten different proteins. These proteins are responsible for everything in the body, from eye color and ear shape to personality and behavior.

Genes and Addiction

Sometimes genes aren't perfect. A change (called a *mutation*) in just one gene can cause a hereditary disease. *Cystic fibrosis* and *Huntington's disease* are examples of hereditary conditions that can be caused by just one altered gene. Through studies such as the Human Genome Project, the genes behind some of these diseases have been identified, and it is believed that this knowledge will allow more effective treatments to be developed.

Identifying genes that might be responsible for addiction is not that easy. Research has shown that addiction may be caused by mutations of more than one gene. Studies have also found that the possible culprits are not the same in all individuals. These factors mean that identifying a hereditary cause for addiction may take many, many years.

Despite the difficulty of locating target genes, researchers do have an idea of where to look. According to the National Institute on Drug Abuse (NIDA; www. nida.nih.gov), researchers are concentrating on genes that control dopamine, a neurotransmitter that is responsible for the sensation of pleasure.

Nerves and neurons are the primary components of the body's complex communication system. Neurotransmitters act as messengers between the different nerves in your body. If your brain wants your hand to move from its position on your lap to scratch your head, a complex system of nerves has to be activated to send that message. It doesn't seem as though the simple action of scratching

Neurotransmitters are the chemicals that carry messages between nerve cells.

Addiction in America—Society, Psychology, and Heredity 59

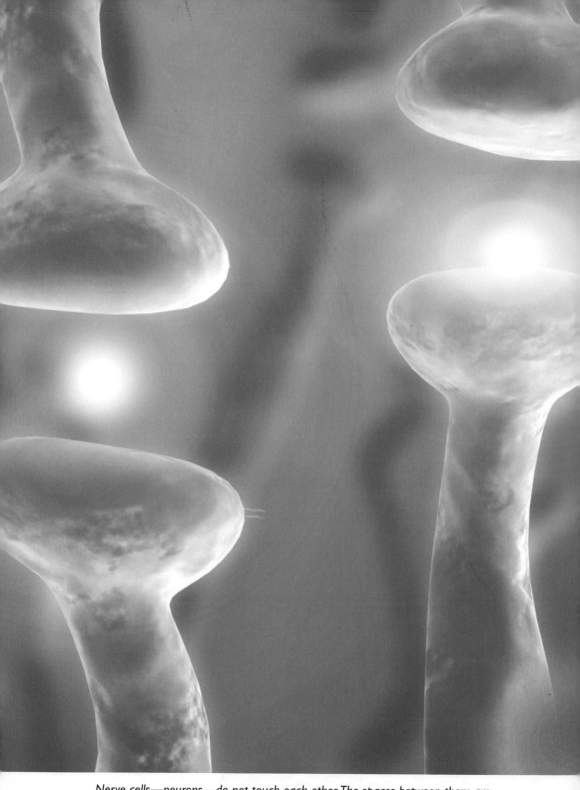

Nerve cells—neurons—do not touch each other. The spaces between them are called synapses.

one's head is all that complicated—but completing even that simple task requires a distinct language to communicate between nerves. The neurotransmitters serve as that language. Neurons do not touch each other, and the area between the neurons is called the synapse. Messages are sent when the impulse reaches the end of the neuron, hops a ride across the synapse on a neurotransmitter, and arrives at the next neuron, and the process continues until the hand scratches the head.

All of the most-abused drugs raise the level of dopamine in the body, increasing the user's sense of pleasure.

Most of scientists' understanding of genetics is based on research done on mice.

When higher levels are artificially produced in the body because of the intake of drugs, the body eventually begins to reduce the amount of dopamine it produces naturally. Many researchers conclude that when the drug-induced levels of dopamine are not present, the individual may feel a significant lack of pleasure. Some individuals will return to drug use to obtain the "high" they have gotten used to. This theory is somewhat confirmed through studies using mice as subjects. Research conducted in mice has led many to conclude that the inability to produce adequate levels of dopamine may lead to addiction in an attempt to achieve pleasure.

Although research in mice is promising, it's a long way from a mouse to a human. There has been some progress in discovering what genes might cause addiction in humans. According to the NIDA, the prime target of researchers is a gene that tells the body to produce catecholo-methyltransferase (COMT), an enzyme that aids in breaking down dopamine. Researchers know that there are two types of COMT—low activity and high activity. In individuals who abuse drugs, genes prompting the high-activity form of COMT are more prevalent.

Determining the genes responsible for addiction is a difficult task and may take many years. To date, most of the research on heredity and addiction has concentrated on alcohol abuse.

Heredity and Alcoholism

Many studies have shown a genetic link in alcoholism. Some researchers contend that up to half of someone's risk factors for developing alcoholism can be attributed to genetics. Genetic studies of alcoholism have found:

• The amygdala, the area of the brain believed to play a role in the emotional aspects of craving, is smaller in those with a family history of alcoholism.

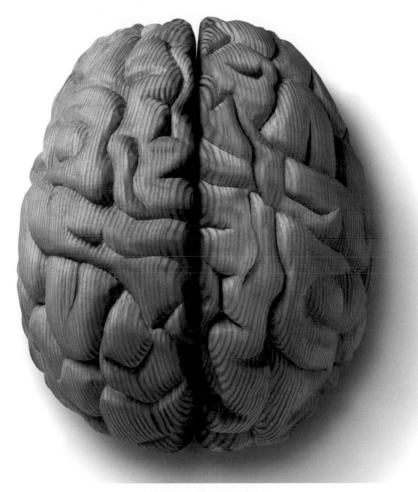

Those who have a genetic predisposition to alcoholism may have differences in their brain structure.

Addiction in America—Society, Psychology, and Heredity 63

- A genetic deficiency of acetaldehyde, found in Asians and Jewish populations, may allow a buildup of acetate after drinking alcohol, which can cause flushing, dizziness, and nausea after drinking, detriments to becoming alcoholic.

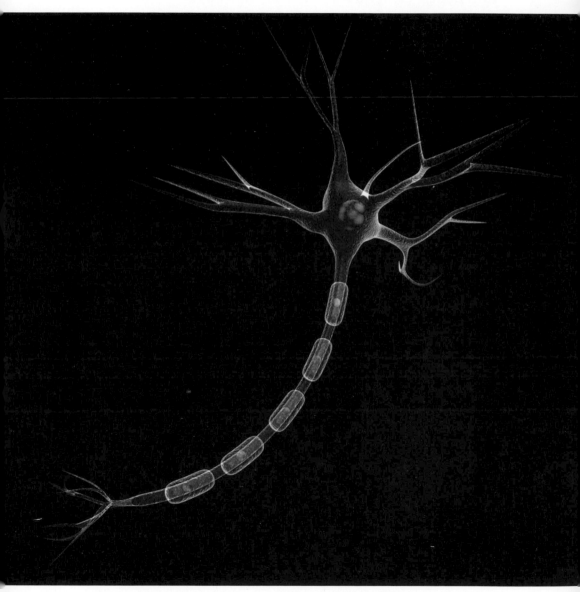

The ability of these tiny cells to communicate with each other may contribute to a tendency to alcoholism.

- Some people who have alcoholism may also have abnormal levels of serotonin, a neurotransmitter. Abnormal serotonin levels are associated with high tolerance levels for alcohol and can affect impulsive behaviors, which can make individuals more likely to drink, and drink a lot.

Researchers studying the predisposition to alcoholism have conducted many twin studies. Identical twins share all genetic material; their DNA is the same, and so they are always the same sex. (Fraternal twins are genetically similar as any other brothers or sisters born to the same parents; these twins can be both boys, both girls, or one of each.) Studies have shown that identical twins of alcoholic parents are more likely than fraternal twins to develop an alcohol addiction. In a study reported on the website www.drugrehabtreatment.com, male identical twins have a 50 percent to 200 percent greater rate of alcohol addiction than fraternal twins. Similar statistics were found for addiction to sedatives, cocaine, stimulants, and opiates.

The influence of heredity extends beyond the birth family. The website www.hazelden.org reports that studies have shown that children of alcoholic parents who are adopted by nonalcoholic individuals have higher rates of alcoholism than children born to nonalcoholic parents and raised by nonalcoholic adoptive or foster parents.

Continuing the Search for a Genetic Cause

Although the task of finding the gene or genes responsible for addiction is a daunting one, scientists continue their search. According to the NIDA, they are using a procedure called a genome-wide scan, which has been

5 Addiction's Effects on Society

For many years, people with extreme pain could often do little more than just suffer through it—or try to at least. Pain management for these individuals was an unfulfilled dream. Some were cancer patients who had to deal with debilitating pain. For others, the pain might have resulted from an injury. In some cases, the pain was so excruciating and constant that they could only find relief when medicated so heavily they appeared "zombie-like."

Then, along came what looked like a miracle. In December 1995, Purdue Pharma, L.P. introduced a product to the U.S. market that promised to help people living with extreme pain. OxyContin®, the brand name for oxycodone hydrochloride (or oxycodone HCL), came in time-release tablets. This time-release dispersal method meant that individuals could take larger dosages, but because the medication was not released immediately, the individual experienced fewer side effects than if the entire dosage was released at once. This meant hours of pain relief before more medication would be needed.

In just four years after it became available on the market, sales of OxyContin in the United States reached $1 billion. Almost six million prescriptions were written for the drug in 2000 alone. Word spread that a wonder-working pain reliever had been discovered, and its success was touted in the media. It wouldn't take long, however, before it got attention for another reason.

The problem with OxyContin was that it worked too well, and individuals looking for an effective high quickly turned to it. The abuse of OxyContin became so common in the rural South that it became known as "Hillbilly Heroin." Pharmacies were robbed, but instead of taking money, thieves took their supply of OxyContin. A drug that had been developed to help people became a *scourge* in many communities, wrecking lives and potentially forever altering the social fabric of that area.

The above story is adapted from a chapter in *Painkillers: Prescription Dependency*, another book in the series Illicit and Misused Drugs. It shows how drugs—even those developed for legitimate medical purposes—can adversely affect communities and society in general. According to the NIDA, in 2002, the cost to society of illicit drug abuse was $181 billion. When costs due to alcohol and tobacco addiction are factored into the equation, the total costs skyrocket to more than $600 *billion* today. These costs include expenses related to health care and criminal justice. The NIDA also reports that each year, about 40 million debilitating illnesses or injuries occur among Americans that can be traced to their use of tobacco, alcohol, or another addictive substance. According to the NIDA, in 2000 an estimated 460,000 deaths were linked to the abuse of illicit drugs and smoking. According to the Partnership at Drugfree.org, alcohol alone kills 75,000 people each year.

Smoking is one of the leading causes of death in our society.

Addiction in America—Society, Psychology, and Heredity 71

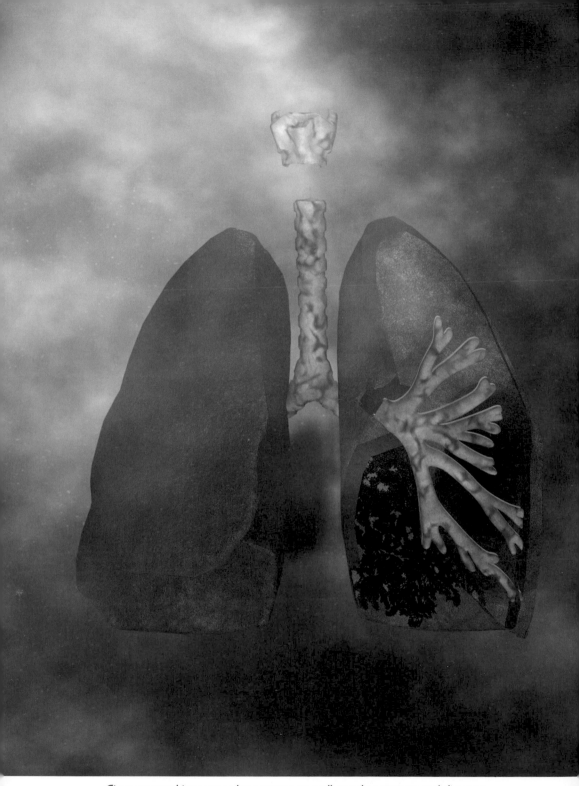

Cigarette smoking causes lung cancer, as well as other cancers and diseases.

Addiction and Health Care

In what might seem like a cosmic irony, substances used to bring extreme happiness can lead to extreme unhealthiness. The NIDA pinpoints alcohol, tobacco, and drug abuse as the cause of more than 500,000 deaths per year, just in the United States. They also contribute to hospital stays, lost workdays, and to the increasing costs of health care. If people with addictions have health insurance, they will most likely use it—sometimes frequently—during the year. This use, on a wide scale, can lead to increased health insurance premiums for everyone. If people with addictions don't have health insurance (and some don't since they are unable to hold a job that provides it), the government and taxpayers end up footing the bill.

But health-care costs are not limited to the individual who has a problem with substance addiction. Some drugs can affect fetuses, leading to premature birth, a lifetime of health problems, or retardation. Secondhand smoke can compromise the health of and even kill those who are exposed to it, even if they have never smoked themselves.

Tobacco and alcohol addictions are prime examples of the health-care costs of addiction.

Tobacco

The American Cancer Society (ACS) estimates that lung cancer will kill 160,000 adults each year; seven out of eight of those individuals will have developed lung cancer because of an addiction to tobacco products. According to the American Lung Association, the direct medical costs of treating lung cancer alone top $5 billion annually. The ACS estimates that more than 12,000 people are diagnosed with *laryngeal* cancer each year, approximately thirty individuals per day. The ACS also estimates that more than 17,000 cases of esophageal cancers are diagnosed each year in the United States. In countries such as China, Iran, India, and the southern region of Africa, places where smoking is prevalent and still acceptable on a wide scale, the rate of tobacco-related esophageal cancer cases each year is ten to one hundred times the rate in the United States.

Canadian statistics indicate that one-fifth of all cancer-related deaths are caused by smoking; more than 47,000 Canadians die each year from smoking. Tobacco-related deaths in the United States are more than eight and a half times that number; it is estimated that more than 400,000 Americans die each year from smoking-related diseases. More than 276,000 males and 142,000 females die from causes attributed to smoking.

FAST FACT

Cigarette smoking causes at least 30 percent of all cancer deaths. It is linked to 80 percent of lung cancer deaths and to more than 90 percent of oral and laryngeal cancers. One half of all cigarette smokers die because of their habit.

Those are just the statistics relating to cancer. But cancer is not the only health issue faced by individuals who smoke tobacco products. **Chronic** obstructive pulmonary disease (COPD) refers to two lung diseases, chronic bronchitis and emphysema. Both diseases restrict the individual's airflow, making normal breathing difficult; in advanced cases, it is not unusual for the individual to require supplemental oxygen. Both diseases often occur together. According to the Ameri-

- Eighty to 90 percent of people with chronic obstructive pulmonary disease (COPD)—a group of lung diseases—have a history of significant tobacco use.
- The Centers for Disease Control and Prevention (CDC) estimates that men and women who smoke are ten times more likely to die of bronchitis and emphysema than those who do not smoke.
- The U.S. Department of Health and Human Services states that the risk of a stroke in people who smoke is 50 percent higher than in those who don't.
- The CDC estimates that tobacco use triples the risk of dying from heart disease and doubles the risk of sudden cardiac death (heart attack).

can Lung Association, COPD is the third-leading cause of death in the United States; in 2007, approximately 12.1 million U.S. adults had COPD. The primary risk factor for developing COPD is smoking tobacco products; secondhand smoke is a factor in some cases of COPD among individuals who have never smoked. An estimated 80 percent to 90 percent of individuals with COPD have a history of smoking, which sometimes continues despite the diagnosis of COPD. Women who smoke are thirteen times more likely to die from COPD than are women who do not smoke. Men who smoke are twelve times more likely to die from COPD than men who do not.

Based on the number of individuals who live with a diagnosis of COPD, it's no wonder that health-care costs associated with COPD are staggering. The American Lung Association estimates that in 2010, national costs for COPD were approximately $49.9 billion: $29.5 billion in direct health-care costs, 8.0 billion in indirect

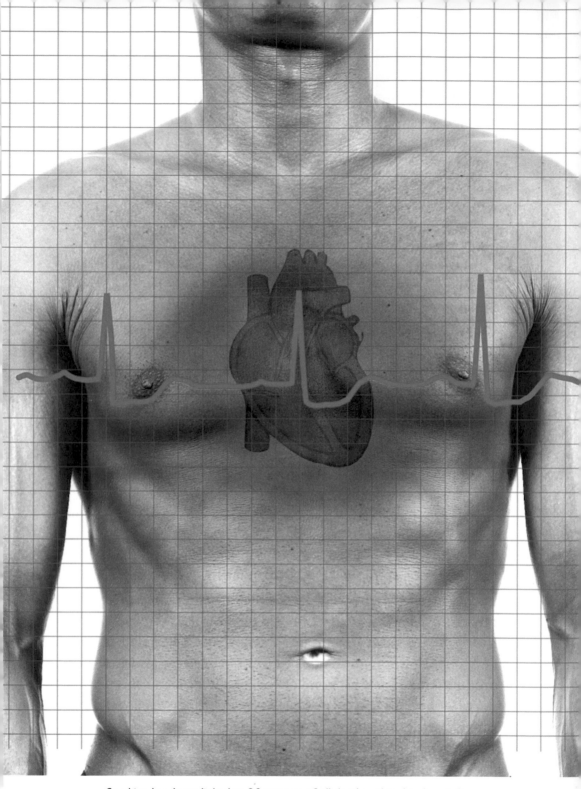

Smoking has been linked to 20 percent of all deaths related to heart disease.

determining all of the ways it affects the body. Some of the ones that are best understood are:

- In general, people who drink regularly have a higher rate of death from injury, violence, and some cancers.
- Frequent, heavy drinking is associated with a higher risk for alcohol-related medical disorders (pancreatitis, upper gastrointestinal bleeding, nerve damage, and impotence) than is episodic drinking or continuous drinking without intoxication.
- As people age, it takes fewer drinks to become intoxicated, and organs can be damaged by smaller amounts of alcohol than in younger people. Also, up to one-half of the one hundred most prescribed drugs for older people react adversely with alcohol.
- Alcohol abusers who require surgery also have an increased risk of *postoperative* complications, including infections, bleeding, insufficient heart and lung functions, and problems with wound healing. Alcohol withdrawal symptoms after surgery may impose further stress on the patient and hinder recuperation.

All these conditions can cause individuals with alcohol addiction to undergo lengthy and multiple hospital stays, have to take medications for chronic conditions, and lose workdays.

Besides the physical effects directly caused by alcoholism, there is the "collateral" damage caused by the addiction. Alcohol is a factor in at least one-third of all motor-vehicle accidents. A blood alcohol content of more than .08 makes one legally impaired, but for some people, a lower level could be just as deadly. Alcohol also makes one vulnerable to injuries from falls and fights.

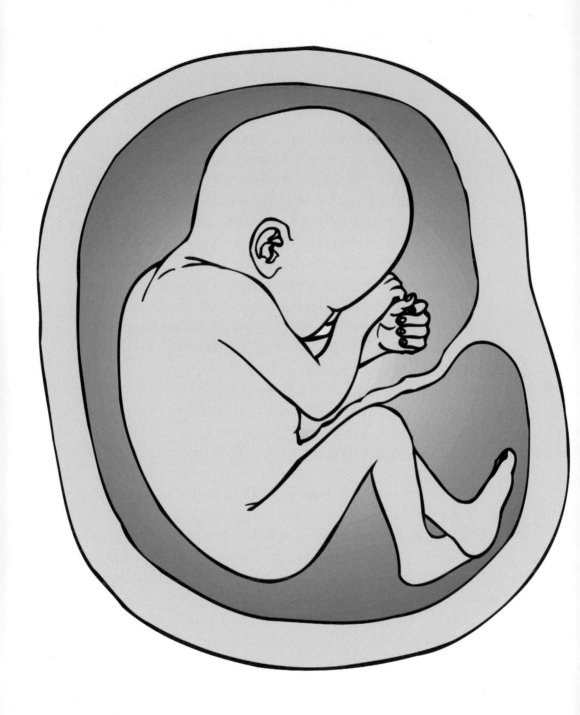

The development of a fetus is affected by the mother's use of tobacco or other drugs.

According to a 2009 article in the CDC's Mortality and Morbidity Weekly report, 24 percent of people who commit suicide show evidence of alcohol intoxication at or above the legal limit. This finding was consistent across all age groups and all ethnicities. The authors suggest that the link is due to the fact that alcohol promotes depression and hopelessness, while also reducing inhibitions, increasing impulsivity, and impairing problem solving.

Domestic violence is a major problem in society, and alcohol exacerbates this situation as well. Research has indicated that a domestic partner with a history of alcohol abuse is the most serious risk factor for women for injury. Children are also at risk of physical injury from an alcohol-abusing parent, and they are also at increased risk of repeating the abusing behavior when they become adults. They have less success at school, are more depressed, have fewer friends, and lower self-esteem than their peers. Those characteristics do not bode well for a fulfilling and happy life as an adult.

Women who continue to drink while pregnant run the very real risk of giving birth to a baby with Fetal Alcohol Syndrome (FAS) or any of the other conditions that can result from a mother continuing to drink during pregnancy. Babies born with this condition may have some, or most, of the following characteristics:

• facial deformities
• neurodevelopment disorder
• a head circumference below the 10th percentile
• intellectual impairment
• memory problems
• delayed development

Alcoholism is not only destructive for the individual; it is also costly to society as a whole.

- *attachment* concerns
- attention deficit disorder
- impaired motor skills
- hyperactivity
- neurosensory hearing loss

Women who drink while pregnant run the risk of damaging their babies' development.

- problems with reasoning and judgment
- learning disabilities
- inability to appreciate consequences
- impaired visual/spatial skills

The Special Case of HIV/AIDS

Many illicit and misused substances can increase the possibility of contracting HIV/AIDS. HIV stands for the human immunodeficiency virus, a retrovirus. Retroviruses integrate and take over a cell's own genetic material. Once taken over, the new cell, now infected with HIV, begins to produce new HIV retroviruses. HIV replicates in the T cells, the body's main defense against illness, and eventually kills them. HIV is only spread through:

- sexual contact from unprotected (without using a condom) vaginal or anal sex
- direct inoculation of the virus through contaminated needles
- contaminated blood products/transplanted organs (In the United States, all donated blood has been tested for HIV since 1985.)
- from an infected mother passing the virus to her developing fetus during birth or through her breast milk

The first one to three months after a person is infected with the HIV virus is when that person is most infectious (that is, the amount of virus in her system is at its highest and T-cell counts are at their lowest). During this time, the body has not had time to react to the virus and produce an adequate immune response to start suppressing HIV. More and more HIV viruses are produced and then released by a process known as budding. This means that

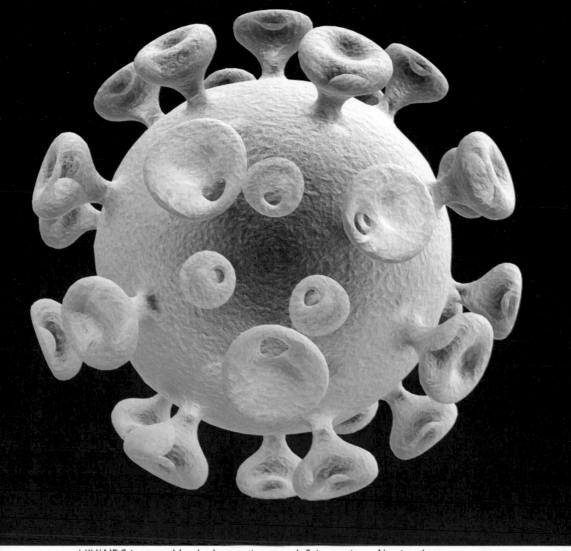

HIV/AIDS is spread by the human immunodeficiency virus. Abusing drugs makes a person's chances of contracting this virus greater.

when someone becomes infected with the HIV virus, it begins to attack her immune system. This process is not visible, and a person who is infected can look and feel perfectly well for many years; she may not even know that she is infected. As the immune system weakens, however, the person will become more vulnerable to illnesses that the immune system would normally have been able to fight. As time goes by, individuals with HIV are likely to become ill more often and develop AIDS.

AIDS stands for acquired immunodeficiency syndrome. When HIV infection becomes advanced, it often is referred to as AIDS. It is characterized by the appearance of *opportunistic infections* that take advantage of a weakened immune system and include:

- pneumocystis carinii pneumonia, a form of pneumonia found almost exclusively in people with compromised immune systems

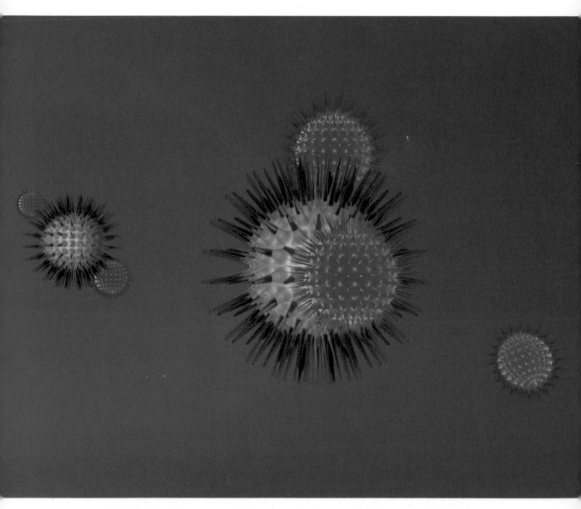

HIV/AIDS weakens a person's immune system, making her more vulnerable to the invasion of other pathogens.

HIV/AIDS and hepatitis can be spread when drug users share needles.

- toxoplasmosis
- tuberculosis
- extreme weight loss and wasting, often made worse by diarrhea
- meningitis and other brain infections
- fungal infections
- syphilis
- malignancies such as lymphoma, cervical cancer, and Kaposi's sarcoma

AIDS derived its name because:

- It is "acquired"; in other words, it is a condition that has to be contracted; it has to be "caught," as it is not inherited.

- It affects the body's immune system, the part of the body that fights off diseases.
- It is considered a "deficiency" because it makes the immune system stop working properly.
- It was originally considered a syndrome because people with AIDS experience a number of different symptoms and opportunistic diseases.

Although nearly everyone in the world knows the term acquired immunodeficiency syndrome or AIDS, this condition is actually a disease and not a syndrome. A syndrome is commonly used to refer to collections of symptoms that do not have an easily identifiable cause; when the term AIDS was first used, doctors were only aware of the late stages of the disease and did not fully understand its mechanisms. A more current name for the condition, regardless of an AIDS diagnosis, is HIV disease. This name is more accurate because it refers to the pathogen that causes AIDS and encompasses all the condition's stages, from infection to the deterioration of the immune system and the onset of opportunistic diseases.

Another Killer

Sharing equipment and having unprotected sexual intercourse can also pass on infections such as hepatitis B and C from one person to another. Hepatitis B is a serious disease caused by a virus that attacks the liver. The virus, which is called hepatitis B virus (HBV), can cause lifelong infection, cirrhosis (scarring) of the liver, liver cancer, liver failure, and death. Hepatitis C is a liver disease caused by the hepatitis C virus (HCV), which is found in the blood of persons who have the disease. HCV is spread by contact with the blood of an infected person. A drop of blood so minuscule that the human eye cannot detect it may contain hundreds or even thousands of hepatitis B and/or C particles. Even meticulous cleaning may not totally eradicate from a needle the viruses that cause these serious liver diseases.

However, AIDS is still the name that most people use to refer to the immune deficiency caused by HIV.

For individuals who inject drugs, the possibility of contracting HIV is very high if they share needles, and many people with addiction share and reuse needles to save money. But sharing needles is not the only way HIV/AIDS can be transmitted. As mentioned above, unprotected sex with someone who has HIV is another way to spread HIV/AIDS. When someone abuses an illicit substance or has too much to drink, his inhibitions can be diminished. Things he might never have considered doing sober don't seem that wild in his intoxicated state. Precautions that he might have insisted on when sober may not even enter his mind.

Great strides have been made in treating medical conditions such

FAST FACT

According to the NIDA:

- Injection drug use is the third most common category of transmission for HIV.

- An estimated one-half of pediatric AIDS cases result from injection drug use or sexual intercourse with injection drug users by the child's mother.

- Children whose mothers used cocaine during pregnancy are more likely to require special education programs; millions are spent each year on special education services in the United States.

- Thirty-one percent of the homeless in the United States are addicted to drugs or alcohol.

as HIV/AIDS, and individuals with HIV/AIDS are living longer and with a higher quality of life than those infected during its early hist-ory. Still, the individuals may find themselves facing long and multiple hospital-izations with prescrip-tions for a multitude of expensive medica-tions. Some will find that their illness re-quires that they miss a great deal of work.

Addiction and Crime

The 2009 Moni-toring the Future Study (MTF) indi-cated that, in gen-eral, drug use among eighth-, tenth-, and twelfth-graders had decreased, the preva-lence of nonmedical use of prescription medication (espe-cially pain relievers) among teens and adults was on the in-crease. The National Survey on Drug Use and Health (NSDUH) defines nonmedical use as oc-curring when an individual takes prescription medications that were not prescribed for her, or takes the medication only for the feeling—the high—that results from taking it.

Many individuals looking for a high resort to committing crimes to pay for their habit. According to the NIDA, as many as 60 percent of individuals incarcerated in federal prisons are there for drug-related crimes. For example, the number of crimes surrounding prescription painkillers such as OxyContin has increased dramatically. In 2002, the *Charlotte Observer* reported that a man in Myrtle Beach, South Carolina, robbed a pharmacy at gunpoint, but he didn't want money; he demanded Oxy-Contin. A former high school teacher in Concord, North Carolina, was arrested and charged with attempting to hire a hit man to murder individuals who still owed him money for OxyContin. In Columbus County, North Carolina, thirty-two people were accused of selling their personal Medicaid cards to drug dealers, who then billed the state for OxyContin prescriptions. According to a 2002 report by the Office of National Drug Control Policy, most OxyContin-related crimes were robbery, burglary, larceny, and other property crimes. The U.S. Drug En-

Monitoring the Future

Since 1975, the Monitoring the Future (MTF) survey has measured drug, alcohol, and cigarette use and related attitudes among adolescent students nationwide. Survey participants report their drug use behaviors across three time periods: lifetime, past year, and past month. In 2009, over 46,000 students in grades 8, 10, and 12 from 400 public and private schools participated in the survey. The survey is funded by the National Institute on Drug Abuse, a component of the National Institutes of Health, and conducted by the University of Michigan.

This photo shows firearms, cash, and OxyContin seized in a drug raid by the West Virginia State Police.

forcement Administration has reported, however, that gunrunning and the sale of stolen guns has played a role in financing drug dealing of prescription painkillers.

A June 2005 article in the *Saint Paul Pioneer Press* reported that one-fourth of those incarcerated in Minnesota prisons are there because of problems with drug addiction, half to methamphetamine. According to Nanette Schroeder, director of health services for the Minnesota Department of Corrections, 90 percent of those incarcerated have a chemical dependency or a history of one. A police officer quoted in the article says they are obviously trying to support a habit, "and they're tough habits to break."

The United States isn't the only country finding its prison and jail populations increasing due to drug addiction. The Canadian Police Forces reported that drug-related crime in Canada is also on the rise since the early 1990s. In 2007, most of the drug-related crimes involved marijuana, mostly for possession. One in ten homicides was drug related; 60 percent involved cocaine. Another 20 percent involved marijuana.

According to 2004 statistics, it cost $23,183.69 to house one individual in a U.S. Bureau of Prisons facility. When incarcerated in a community correctional facility, the cost dropped to $19,087.94. In federal prisons, inmates are expected to contribute 25 percent of their income, called an incarceration fee, to help offset the cost of their imprisonment.

If you're the victim of a crime committed by someone addicted to drugs, or if you read statistics about how many are incarcerated, it's fairly easy to understand the cost of crime-related addiction on society. But the cost effects extend beyond the one committing the crime. The person who suffered the crime might have lost something with a financial value, but there's also the emotional cost of crime. Many crime victims find that they are unable to sleep, suffer from anxiety, and have other problems dealing with their ordeal. Counseling and medication can be beneficial to many—but these aids cost money.

Even those who had nothing to do with the crime can feel its results. Many times the individuals who committed the crimes have families they helped support. When those families lose the income—however

Addiction contributes to crime, which increases incarceration rates, which in turn raises the costs to North American society.

obtained—they have to turn elsewhere. The lucky ones have other means of support—legal ones such as jobs. Others turn to other family members or to the welfare system for help.

No one escapes the costs of addiction. It is to everyone's benefit, therefore, to stop addiction in its tracks.

 # Stopping Addiction

I didn't start out to be an addict. I don't think anyone does. But, it just seemed to get away from me. I wanted more and more. . . . It didn't seem as though I could get enough. So, I decided to stop using coke right then and there . . . cold turkey. Through the grace of God, it worked. For a while, anyway. But then I started getting those cravings again, and there didn't seem to be anything I could do to make them go away—except take a hit. So I did. Then I took another and another until I was hooked again. By this time, my mom had had enough. She dragged me to rehab. That was four years ago, and I still thank her every day. (Matthew, age twenty-one)

Call me naive, but that TV commercial, you know, where they crack the egg into the frying pan and this guy's voice goes "Here's your brain on drugs," well, that one really scared me. I don't know why. When I think back on it, it really wasn't all the scary. There was just something about it that scared the crap out of me. I never wanted to try drugs after that—and I am proud to say I never did. (Callie Ann, age eighteen)

These are snippets from a conversation that took place about drug addiction in an Internet chat room. Matthew and Callie are examples of two tools used to stop addiction—treatment and education.

Addiction and Treatment

Except in extremely rare cases (and television shows and movies), most people who become addicted to a substance do so on their own; no one forces them to take—or keep taking—a drug or to drink alcoholic beverages. This fact leads many with substance addiction, like Matthew, to believe that they can beat their addiction on their own. Sadly, this generally results in repeated failures at sobriety, at least in the long run.

So, why *can't* individuals conquer addiction on their own? If the drug use has only occurred for a short time, they often can. But, the longer an individual has been addicted to the substance, the less likely it is that he can permanently abstain from using the substance without the help of some kind of a treatment program. Researchers studying drugs and addiction have discovered that when drugs are used over a long period, serious changes occur in how the brain functions. Some of these changes, including the perceived need to continue using the substance, can continue long after the person has stopped taking the drug or substance. If the individual has not learned ways to cope with the continuing cravings to use the drug or substance, he will probably relapse.

It's not just the drug's long-term effects on the brain that can doom individual attempts at sobriety. For many addicted to drugs and alcohol, the entire drug-taking experience is a time to socialize with friends. Some individuals

Teens are particularly susceptible to peer pressure.

Addiction in America—Society, Psychology, and Heredity 99

do not have the strength to stand up to their friends, family, or coworkers and be the only one not using drugs or alcohol. It's not easy to be the only one not doing something. Peer pressure, especially when combined with changes the substance might have caused in the brain, can make abstinence a non-winnable war.

The right treatment program depends on the substance of addiction and characteristics (such as age) of the individual with the addiction. There are, however, characteristics common to most treatment programs. The first step

According to Veterans Affairs Canada (www.vac-acc.gc.ca/clients/sub.cfm?source=health/wellness/9), someone may have a problem with drugs if they:

• drink alcohol or use drugs in secret
• suffer blackouts
• have headaches or hangovers
• consume quickly and more often.

The problem may be addiction if any of the following can be answered by yes:

• Are you having problems with any part of your life? Physical health? Work? Family? Mental health? Your social or spiritual life?
• Do you know when to stop drinking? Do you often drink too much and become intoxicated? Do you binge drink?
• Do you have withdrawal symptoms such as shakiness, irritability or seizures when you stop drinking or using drugs?
• Are you using illegal drugs or having your drugs prescribed by more than one doctor?
• Has your drug use increased since you first started using them?
• Are you spending more and more time thinking about where the money for your next drinks or drugs will come from?

Detoxification is done in a medically supervised environment, such as a hospital.

in overcoming any addiction is to admit there *is* a problem, that one is an addict. In some ways, this may be one of the hardest of a series of incredibly hard steps. But it is impossible to finish the journey to sobriety without taking that first step of admitting to being an addict. Many people with addictions complete programs without using the word "addict" to describe themselves, but these individuals often find themselves doing multiple stints in rehab.

The most effective method of addiction treatment involves a multidisciplinary approach—and it doesn't happen over night.

Detoxification

When one decides to break free from addiction, the body must go through a process of withdrawal to rid itself of the toxic substances of the drug. Through a medically supervised process called detoxification, the individual goes through some or all of the withdrawal symptoms specific to the substance of addiction. How long withdrawal lasts depends on how much and what type of drug was taken. For people who are addicted to prescription painkillers, for example, the detoxification process generally takes place in a hospital or drug treatment facility.

For someone who is dependent on drugs, this process might be enough to prevent further misuse. But the person who is addicted to drugs needs follow-up treatment; studies have shown that most people with addictions will return to their previous behaviors if treatment ends with the detoxification phase. The two primary methods for treating addiction are behavioral and pharmacological.

Behavioral Treatment Programs

Put simply, behavioral treatment programs teach people with addictions to change their behaviors so they are less likely to repeat those that led to addiction in the first place. Well, that's the theory anyway. Unfortunately, nothing about addiction is simple. Though behavioral treatment programs do help those with addictions find ways to avoid behaviors that can cause a relapse, they also must help them discover what led to those behaviors initially. Cognitive-behavioral therapy helps the individuals recognize how thought patterns influence behaviors. During therapy, individuals learn how to change negative thought patterns, thereby changing behaviors. Individual and family therapy can help the person with addiction and those around her learn how to live as and with a recovering addict. Therapy can also help the addicted individual and her friends and family handle relapses; most people do relapse at some point during recovery.

Behavioral treatment programs also help those with addictions handle life without the drug, including the

What Do Rehab Programs Accomplish?

Abstinence

In many cases it seems that as long as the substance is in the blood stream, thinking remains distorted. Often during the first days or weeks of total abstinence, we see a gradual clearing of thinking processes. This is a complex psychological and biological phenomenon, and is one of the elements that inpatient programs are able to provide by making sure the patient is fully detoxified and remains abstinent during his or her stay.

Removal of Denial

In some cases, when someone other than the patient, such as a parent, employer, or other authority, is convinced there is a problem, but the addict is not yet sure, voluntary attendance at a rehab program will provide enough clarification to remove this basic denial. Even those who are convinced they have a problem with substances usually don't admit to themselves or others the full extent of the addiction. Rehab uses group process to identify and help the individual to let go of these expectable forms of denial.

Removal of Isolation

As addictions progress, relationships deteriorate in quality. However, the bonds between fellow recovering people are widely recognized as one of the few forces powerful enough to keep recovery on track. The rehab experience, whether it is inpatient or outpatient involves in-depth sharing in a group setting. This kind of sharing creates strong interpersonal bonds among group members. These bonds help to form a support system that will be powerful enough to sustain the individual during the first months of abstinence.

"Basic Training"

Basic training is a good way to think of the experience of rehab. Soldiers need a rapid course to give them the basic knowledge and skills they will need to fight in a war. Some kinds of learning need to be practiced so well that you can do them without thinking. In addition to the learning, trainees become physically fit, and perhaps most important, form emotional bonds that help keep up morale when the going is hard.

(Source: *Partnership for a Drug-Free America*)

sometimes-painful cravings for the drug. If the individual is addicted to prescription pain medication, for example, he must also learn how to deal with pain. Even if his introduction to prescription painkillers was not the result of a medical need, there may come a time when pain medications will be necessary. He needs to know how to handle that situation to lessen the possibility that he will relapse. If the drug was something that might be medically necessary at some point (like prescription painkillers) or something the person might have a difficult time avoiding (such as over-the-counter medications), treat-

Painkillers are hard to avoid forever; sooner or later, an individual will probably need to take them for legitimate reasons, which may put him at risk for relapsing into addiction.

ment must contain methods for handling those situations. Otherwise, the likelihood of a successful recovery is compromised. No matter what substance was abused, the best treatment results are achieved when the individual practices abstinence from the substance.

Behavioral treatment programs often begin with a period of inpatient treatment. Depending on the length, severity, and drug of addiction, inpatient treatment can be short-term (usually a minimum of thirty days) or long-term residential. At first, some programs allow inpatients to have minimal—if any—contact with the "outside world." Patients concentrate on learning about themselves and their relationship with the drug. Later, family and perhaps close friends are encouraged to participate in the treatment program.

Pharmacological Treatment Programs

For some addictions, medications are effective treatment tools. They are used in both inpatient and outpatient settings. Addictions to prescription painkillers and alcohol, for example, can be treated with medications.

Most treatment programs use a combination of behavioral treatment and pharmacological methods. Individuals are also encouraged to supplement their programs with support groups. In some cases, participation begins while the individual is still an inpatient.

Support Groups

The individual fighting an addiction may feel as though he is the only person who has experienced what he's going through. His addiction may have put a strain on his relationship with nondrug-using friends and relatives. He may find it difficult to relate to anyone about how he's feeling. This is where support groups may be a valuable resource.

Alcoholics Anonymous

One of the best-known support groups is Alcoholics Anonymous (AA), founded in 1935 with the goal of helping people who have problems with alcohol. Today there are chapters all over the world. Its books and pamphlets are published in more than thirty languages.

Each chapter's program is based on the original twelve steps that have become synonymous with AA. The steps have a spiritual component, to which some people might object, but many studies have proven the value of some form of prayer and meditation to a recovery program. The AA program emphasizes that the Higher Power referred to in the steps does not refer to any particular belief system; it can mean what the individual wants—and needs—it to mean. The twelve steps are:

1. We admitted we were powerless over alcohol—that our lives had become unmanageable.
2. Came to believe that a Power greater than ourselves could restore us to sanity.
3. Made a decision to turn our will and our lives over to the care of God as we understand Him.
4. Made a searching and fearless moral inventory of ourselves.
5. Admitted to God, and to our selves, and to another human being, the exact nature of our wrongs.
6. We're entirely ready to have God remove all these defects of character.
7. Humbly asked Him to remove our shortcomings.

8. Made a list of all persons we had harmed, and became willing to make amends to them all.
9. Made direct amends to such people wherever possible, except when to do so would injure them or others.
10. Continued to take personal inventory and when we were wrong promptly admitted it.
11. Sought through prayer and meditation to improve our conscious contact with God as we understand Him, praying only for knowledge of His will for us and the power to carry that out.
12. Having had a spiritual awakening as the result of these steps, we tried to carry this message to drug addicts and to practice these principles in all our affairs.

AA encourages members to seek spiritual strength as an element of their battle against addiction.

Addiction in America—Society, Psychology, and Heredity 107

AA recognizes the importance of family and friends to the person as she adjusts to and lives life as a recovering alcoholic. Al-Anon and Alateen operate as support groups for friends and families, helping those involved with the recovering alcoholic deal with the changes as well as realize they are not alone on their journey.

The success of AA has led to the development of other twelve-step programs, including Narcotics Anonymous (NA) and Cocaine Anonymous (CA). All are based on the same premises as AA. Though participation in AA

AA suggests that those with addictions use friendships and family relationships as another source of strength.

and other twelve-step program meetings will not guarantee a recovery free from temptation and relapse, they can play an important role in staying sober.

Other Support Groups

For whatever reason, some people don't find twelve-step programs helpful. There are many other support groups in which they can participate. Many hospitals, treatment centers, community centers, and houses of worship offer support groups for individuals working on recovery. Most have a social hour following the meeting, giving people the opportunity to mingle and enjoy refreshments as well as learn how others are coping with recovery.

If someone is shy, uncomfortable talking in groups, ill, or without transportation, these support groups may not work for her. This is where the Internet can play a major role in the recovery process. There is an Internet mailing list, chat room, or group for almost anything anyone can imagine, and this includes recovery from addiction. However, it is very important that one exercise caution when giving out personal information. Though most people who participate in these groups and lists are just seeking information and support, there are some with motives not quite so innocent. Be careful about giving out personal information; in most cases, first names should be enough. Should you decide to meet someone in person, make sure the meeting takes place in a public location, preferably during the day, and ask if you can bring along a friend.

Regardless of whether one attends an in-person support group or participates in a virtual one, care should also be used when assessing the information one gets. What works for one person might not work for someone else.

Education

The best addiction prevention method is to not become addicted in the first place. Educators in many areas have gotten savvy about effective ways to educate students about drugs and their effects.

One of the best-known programs is D.A.R.E. (Drug Abuse Resistance Education). The D.A.R.E. program, which began in Los Angeles in 1983, aims at teaching students from kindergarten through twelfth grade how to avoid drugs and violence, as well as how to resist negative peer pressure. In 2008, 10 million students in the United States, with another 36 million worldwide, participated in the program. Eighty percent of U.S. school districts implement the program, which is led by a police officer, each year.

In recent years, some experts and researchers on drug abuse have questioned success rates claimed by the program. Criticism has centered around lack of follow-up as the students enter later grades. Despite these criticisms, the program has grown and now even includes interactive activities on its Web site.

Ad campaigns can also play a role in education. When it became apparent that the abuse of OxyContin was widespread, for example, the drug's manufacturer stepped in to join the fight to prevent abuse. They created an ad campaign, including school posters and classroom materials, warning about the dangers of prescription drug abuse. The posters pulled no punches, with text such as "Picking your nose at lunch does not count as dessert and *spastic* shaking caused by abusing prescription drugs is creepy," and to describe side effects of prescription drug abuse, imagery of "explosive diarrhea" and "blowing chunks." Of course, it is possible to second-guess the company's

D.A.R.E. and other school-based programs try to fight addiction through educational programs.

Addiction in America—Society, Psychology, and Heredity 111

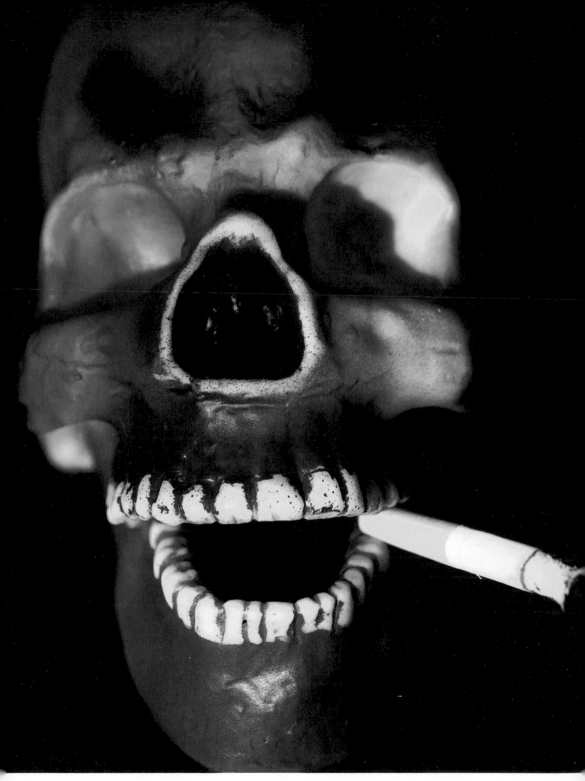

Anti-smoking ads often use dramatic images to convey their message.

motives. After all, many people were calling for the drug's removal from the market.

Anti-smoking campaigns have relied heavily on television spots. The first ads, paid for by the American Lung Association and the American Cancer Society, appeared on television by 1967. In 1999, tobacco companies got involved in television campaigns—though not exactly by choice. As part of the Master Settlement Agreement between the tobacco industry and attorneys general of forty-six states and five territories, the American Legacy Foundation was created to encourage children to never begin smoking and to help individuals who already did smoke quit. The tobacco industry contributes to Legacy, and Legacy in turn uses the funds it receives for a variety of anti-smoking campaigns, including television ads called "truth" ads.

Do the ads work? It appears they do—sometimes. According to a 2002 study published in the *American Journal of Public Health*, the truth ads produced by Legacy reduced the number of children and teen smokers by 300,000 between 2000 and 2002. However, so-called truth ads created by tobacco company Philip Morris in a campaign called "Think. Don't Smoke" seemed to have had the opposite affect. Another article published in the *American Journal of Public Health*, this one in 2006, reported that the Morris campaign and others similar to it actually encouraged teens to smoke. Using data from Nielsen Media Research, researchers studied the impact of those ads on children and adolescents between the ages of twelve and seventeen in the seventy-five largest media markets in the United States. Melanie Wakefield, the study's head researcher, reported, "Tobacco-sponsored ads targeted at youth have no impact, and those targeted at parents

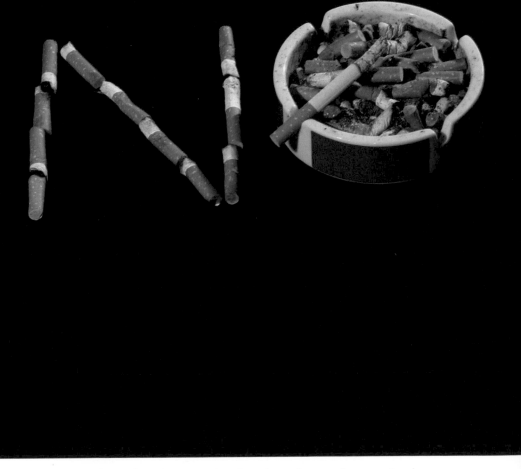

Anti-smoking advertising campaigns have been shown to have varying degrees of success.

seem to have an adverse effect on students who are in their middle and later teenage years." According to the researchers, these ads' purpose is not to prevent smoking but to merely delay it until the individual is an adult. In the end, researchers conclude, parents' influence is the most effective way to keep kids from smoking.

But educational programs do not always have to come from adults and officials. Teenagers in Whitesburg, Kentucky, weren't willing to wait for adults to do something to convince children and other teens to stay off of Oxy-Contin. Working with Appalshop, a cultural center, they produced a documentary about the perils of OxyContin abuse. The documentary, *Because of OxyContin*, featured real-life abusers of the drug telling personal stories of how abusing the drug affected their lives. Included in the documentary was a woman from southwest Virginia who blamed the drug for her losing a child, contracting hepatitis, and possibly becoming infected with HIV.

Legislation

Whether passing laws can truly be considered a method of stopping addiction, local, state, and federal legislatures are being encouraged by their constituents to pass legislation increasing criminal penalties for drug possession and trafficking.

The U.S. Department of Justice Drug Enforcement Administration (DEA) categorizes drugs according to their potential for abuse and whether they have an accepted medical use. Penalties for possession and sale are partly based on where the drug falls on the DEA's Drug Schedule.

Faced with losing federal highway funds, states have increased the age at which individuals can legally buy

U.S. Department of Justice Drug Enforcement Administration

Schedule I

- The drug or other substance has a high potential for abuse.
- The drug or other substance has no currently accepted medical use in treatment in the United States.
- There is a lack of accepted safety for use of the drug or other substance under medical supervision.
- Some Schedule I substances are heroin, LSD, and marijuana.

Schedule II

- The drug or other substance has a high potential for abuse.
- The drug or other substance has a currently accepted medical use in treatment in the United States or a currently accepted medical use with severe restrictions.
- Abuse of the drug or other substance may lead to severe psychological or physical dependence.
- Schedule II substances include morphine, PCP, cocaine, methadone, and methamphetamine.

Schedule III

- The drug or other substance has a potential for abuse less than the drugs or other substances in Schedules I and II.
- The drug or other substance has a currently accepted medical use in treatment in the United States.
- Abuse of the drug or other substance may lead to moderate or low physical dependence or high psychological dependence.
- Anabolic steroids, codeine and hydrocodone with aspirin or Tylenol, and some barbiturates are Schedule III substances.

Schedule IV

- The drug or other substance has a low potential for abuse relative to the drugs or other substances in Schedule III.
- The drug or other substance has a currently accepted medical use in treatment in the United States.
- Abuse of the drug or other substance may lead to limited physical dependence or psychological dependence relative to the drugs or other substances in Schedule III.
- Included in Schedule IV are Darvon, Talwin, Equanil, Valium, and Xanax.

Schedule V

- The drug or other substance has a low potential for abuse relative to the drugs or other substances in Schedule IV.
- The drug or other substance has a currently accepted medical use in treatment in the United States.
- Abuse of the drug or other substance may lead to limited physical dependence or psychological dependence relative to the drugs or other substances in Schedule IV.
- Over-the-counter cough medicines with codeine are classified in Schedule V.

(*Source*: www.dea.gov)

and consume alcoholic beverages. At the same time, most have lowered the legally intoxicated level to 0.08. Drivers who violate the law face increasingly stiffer sentences, including the potential for long sentences should they be responsible for a fatal vehicle accident.

Whatever its cause, whatever form it takes, and whatever methods are used to combat it, addiction affects everyone—it's everyone's problem, and everyone must be involved in the solution.

Glossary

adverse: Negative.

attachment: A psychological bond, as between mother and child.

beta-blockers: Drugs used to regulate the activity of the heart, especially in the treatment of high blood pressure, by suppressing the activity of beta-receptors.

blood–brain barrier: A naturally occurring barrier created by the modification of brain capillaries that prevents many substances from leaving the bloodstream and entering the brain tissue.

chronic: Long term or frequently recurring.

cohesive: Unified.

composite: Made up of different parts.

conduct disorders: A group of childhood/adolescent disturbances of repetitive and persistent antisocial actions that violate the rights of others.

consummate: Possessing or showing a quality to the highest degree.

controversial: Having to do with a topic that causes disagreement and arguments.

cortisone: A hormone secreted by the adrenal gland and used to treat rheumatoid arthritis and allergies.

cystic fibrosis: A hereditary disease starting in infancy that affects various glands and results in secretion of thick mucus that blocks internal passages including the lungs.

emulate: Try to equal someone or something.

endorphins: Substances in the brain that attach to the same cell receptors that morphine does, and that are released when severe injury occurs, abolishing all sensation of pain.

euphoria: A feeling of great joy, excitement, or well-being.

exacerbated: Made worse.

Huntington's disease: A hereditary disease that usually appears in middle age and is characterized by symptoms including increasing mobility difficulties and dementia.

hypothalamus: The central part of the underside of the brain that is responsible for controlling involuntary functions.

hypotheses: Tentative explanations for a phenomenon, used as the basis for further investigations.

hypothesized: Made a hypothesis.

laryngeal: Pertaining to the larynx (voice box).

morbidity: The presence of illness or disease.

mortality: The number of deaths that occur at a given time, in a given group, or from a given cause.

mutation: A random change in a gene or chromosome that results in a new trait or characteristic that can be inherited by succeeding generations.

opportunistic infections: Illnesses or disease that occur in persons with weak immune systems due to AIDS, cancer, or immunosuppressive drugs such as chemotherapy.

paranoia: A psychosis involving distrustfulness of others and feelings of persecution.

Parkinson's disease: An incurable nervous disorder characterized by trembling hands, lifeless face, monotone voice, and a slow, shuffling walk.

peer group: A social group consisting of people who are equal in such respects as age, education, or social class.

peptides: Chemical compounds whose amino acids have chemical bonds between carboxyl and amino groups.

pharmacology: The study of drugs, including their sources, chemistry, production, use in treating disease, and side effects.

postoperative: Following a surgery.

predisposition: The tendency to develop a disease or condition.

productivity: The ability to produce goods or services.

propensity: The tendency to exhibit a particular behavior.

psychoactive: Used to describe drugs having a significant effect on mood or behavior.

purveyors: Suppliers of something.

rationale: The reasoning or principle that underlies or explains a particular course of action.

repressed memories: Recollections of an experience, especially a traumatic one, that are pushed into the subconscious, out of conscious awareness, because of the pain they cause.

scourge: Something seen as an agent of punishment or destruction.

spastic: Affected with involuntary and abnormal muscle contraction.

symptomatic: Having the characteristics of a particular disease or disorder.

touting: Praising or recommending someone or something enthusiastically.

Further Reading

Bindas, Traci. *Really, I'm Not the Only One? Understanding and Coping with Chemical Dependency in the Family.* Minneapolis, Minn.: Educational Media Corporation, 2006.

Esherick, Joan. *Dying for Acceptance: A Teen's Guide to Drug- and Alcohol-Related Health Issues.* Broomall, Pa.: Mason Crest, 2005.

Gaughen, Shasta. *Teen Addiction.* Farmington Hills, Mich.: Greenhaven Press, 2001.

Gerdes, Louise I. *Opposing Viewpoints: Addiction.* Farmington Hills, Mich.: Greenhaven Press, 2004.

Hyde, Margaret O. *Drugs 101.* Minneapolis, Minn.: 21st Century, 2003.

Libal, Joyce. *Drug Therapy and Substance-Related Disorders.* Broomall, Pa.: Mason Crest, 2004.

Marcovitz, Hal. *Drug & Alcohol Abuse.* Broomall, Pa.: Mason Crest, 2006.

Mirman, Heather Moehn. *Issues in Drug Abuse.* Farmington Hills, Mich.: Lucent, 2005.

Muqoz, Mercedes (ed.). *What Causes Addiction?* Farmington Hills, Mich.: Greenhaven Press, 2005.

Mur, Cindy. *Drug Testing.* Farmington Hills, Mich.: Greenhaven Press, 2006.

Papa, Susan. *Addiction.* Farmington Hills, Mich.: Thomson Gale, 2001.

Raczek, Linda Theresa. *Teen Issues: Teen Addiction.* Farmington Hills, Mich.: Lucent, 2003.

Sheen, Barbara. *Chemical Dependency.* Farmington Hills, Mich.: Lucent, 2003.

Walker, Ida. *Painkillers: Prescription Dependency.* Broomall, Pa.: Mason Crest, 2008.

For More Information

AddictionInfo.com
www.addictioninfo.org/categories/Help-Yourself-Addiction-Tools/
Addiction-Theories

Alcohol and Other Drug Information for Teens
www.child.net/drugalc.htm

Alcoholics Anonymous
www.alcoholics-anonymous.org

American Lung Association
www.lungusa.org

D.A.R.E. Program
www.dare.com

Genetic Science Learning Center
learn.genetics.utah.edu

Narcotics Anonymous
www.na.org

Partnership for a Drug-Free America
www.drugfree.org

Silent Treatment: Addiction in America
www.silenttreatment.info/index.html

Teen Drug Abuse
www.teendrugabuse.us/teen_addiction.html

The websites listed on this page were active at the time of publication. The publisher is not responsible for websites that have changed their addresses or discontinued operation since the date of publication. The publisher will review and update the website list upon each reprint.

Bibliography

Boddiger, D. "Battling Addiction." *Lancet* 364(2004): 923–924.

Koop, C. E. "Drug Addiction in America: Challenges and Opportunities." *Military Medicine* 168(2003): viii–xvi.

Levine, Harry G. "The Discovery of Addiction: Changing Conceptions of Habitual Drunkenness in America." *Journal of Studies on Alcohol* 15(1978): 493–506.

Melo, Frederick. "Addictions Fuel Crime, Elude Answers: From Drugs to Gambling, Compulsive Behavior Abounds, but Understanding and Treatment Lag." Saint Paul (Minnesota) *Pioneer Press*, June 6, 2005.

Reuter, P., and H. Pollack. "How Much Can Treatment Reduce National Drug Problems?" *Addiction* 101(2006): 341–347.

Ridenour, Ty A., Stephanie T. Lanza, Eric C. Donny, and Duncan B. Clark. "Different Lengths of Times for Progressions in Adolescent Substance Involvement." *Addictive Behaviors* 31(2006): 962–963.

Stairway to Recovery. "How Society Pays." http://www.uphs.upenn.edu/addiction/berman/society.html.

Stairway to Recovery. "The Role of Genetics in Addiction." http://www.uphs.upenn.edu/addiction/berman/genetic.html.

Stanton Peele and Bruce K. Alexander. "The Meaning of Addiction." http://www.peele.net/lib/moa3.html.

White, William L. "Addiction as a Disease." *Counselor* 1(October 2000): 46–51, 73.

Index

Picture Credits

Amaxim–Fotolia: p. 80
Amikishiyev, Elnur–Fotolia: p. 10
Apito, Bryan–Fotolia: p. 61
Barkaya, Galina–Fotolia: p. 99
Billyfoto: p. 63
Cairon, Jose Vicente–Fotolia: p. 72
Doucet, Michelle L. –Fotolia: p. 107
Gavin, Nicola–Fotolia: p. 20
Girton, Andy–Fotolia: p. 40
Jupiter Images: pp. 41, 42, 44, 47, 48, 68, 71
Kaulitzki, Sabastian–Fotolia: pp. 59, 60
Lee, Taewoon–Fotolia: p. 78
Matilda–Fotolia: p. 18
Mazur, Boguslaw–Fotolia: p. 76
Oates, Lou–Fotolia: p. 94
Pargeter, Kirsty–Fotolia: pp. 87, 108
Phan, Anh–Fotolia: p. 114
Risteski, Goce–Fotolia: p. 52
Rolff, Bruce–Fotolia: p. 96
Rothstein, Scott–Fotolia: pp. 104, 112
Serpault, Cyril–Fotolia: p. 82
Sgame: pp. 64, 85
Spectral–Fotolia: p. 86
StockphotoNYC: p. 8
Swanson, Lorraine–Fotolia: p. 111
Trojanowski, Tomasz–Fotolia: pp. 28, 77
Van Den Berg, Simone–Fotolia: p. 24
Varela, Felipe–Fotolia: p. 49
Vella, Laurent–Fotolia: p. 23
Walsh, Erika–Fotolia: p. 50
Warchol, Bill: p. 66
West Virginia State Police: p. 92
Young, Kelly–Fotolia: p. 101

Author and Consultant Biographies

Author

Ida Walker is a graduate of the University of Northern Iowa and did graduate work at Syracuse University. The author of several non-fiction books for young adults, she currently lives in Upstate New York.

Series Consultant

Jack E. Henningfield, Ph.D., is a professor at the Johns Hopkins University School of Medicine, and he is also Vice President for Research and Health Policy at Pinney Associates, a consulting firm in Bethesda, Maryland, that specializes in science policy and regulatory issues concerning public health, medications development, and behavior-focused disease management. Dr. Henningfield has contributed information relating to addiction to numerous reports of the U.S. Surgeon General, the National Academy of Sciences, and the World Health Organization.